DIRECTORY OF ILLUSTRATION

SERBIN COMMUNICATIONS, INC.
SANTA BARBARA, CALIFORNIA

PUBLISHER/EDITOR
Glen Robert Serbin

ART DIRECTOR/DESIGN
Mehosh Dziadzio

MANAGING EDITOR
Margie Middleton

ADVERTISING DIRECTOR
John Jimenez

ADVERTISING STAFF
Brian Dunn
Holly Schwartz
Steve Travis
Mara Tucker

PRODUCTION COORDINATOR
Monie DeWitt

PRODUCTION STAFF
Adine Maron
Frank Becker

EDITORIAL ASSISTANT
Dori Hoke

ACCOUNTING
Fred Gaeden C.P.A.

BOOKKEEPING
Soans and Associates

GRAPHIC ARTISTS GUILD LIAISON
Simms Taback

COVER DESIGN
Mark Riedy
Scott Hull & Assoc.
68 East Franklin Street
Dayton, Ohio 45459
513 433-8383
212 966-3604

TYPOGRAPHER
The TypeStudio
Tom Buhl

PRINTER
Dai Nippon, Tokyo

**DISTRIBUTORS TO THE TRADE
IN UNITED STATES AND CANADA**
Watson-Guptill Publications
1515 Broadway
New York, New York 10036

WORLDWIDE DISTRIBUTION
Hearst Publications International
105 Madison Avenue
New York, NY 10016

The DIRECTORY OF ILLUSTRATION Volume 8 is published by Serbin Communications, Inc., 511 Olive Street, Santa Barbara, California 93101. 805-963-0439. © 1991 by Serbin Communications, Inc., All rights reserved. Copyright under International and Pan-American Copyright Convention. Printed in Japan. ISBN 8230-6246-5.

FROM THE PUBLISHER

Welcome to our 8th edition of the DIRECTORY OF ILLUSTRATION. The DIRECTORY OF ILLUSTRATION #8 showcases some of the most talented illustrators in the world. Buyers of professional illustration will find this year's directory to be larger and more comprehensive than Volume 7. In fact, the DIRECTORY OF ILLUSTRATION has grown by 15% this year, for a total of 25% during the last two years. This growth gives the buyer of illustration a more comprehensive and diverse selection of artists.

Our Easy Access Index is located on pages 9 through 15. If you are looking for a specific style or subject, this index will steer you in the right direction. Although the Easy Access Index is a helpful guide, I would suggest that you always call our illustrators for a complete portfolio of their subject range.

This DIRECTORY OF ILLUSTRATION displays the original work of various artists and designers. Intended as a source for buyers of art to identify and contact the talent appropriate to their needs, it is not intended to be a library of swipe art or stock illustration. One may be inspired by the work contained in this volume, but using this as the basis for a new design or layout may be considered copyright infringement in violation of applicable copyright laws.

The test for copyright infringement is "whether an ordinary observer, looking at the original work and the work allegedly copied from it, recognizes that a copying has taken place."*

I hope you will rely on the DIRECTORY OF ILLUSTRATION often, and that you will respect the rights of the artists as you would like others to respect your work.

The DIRECTORY OF ILLUSTRATION is a team project. Without the help of my sales team, production staff and the cooperation of our participating artists, timely completion of this project would have been impossible. I want to thank Paul Basista, Executive Director of the Graphic Artists Guild for his professional advice and support. In addition, I would like to thank Sheri Lee and Danny Pelavin for their contribution to the design of the Graphic Artists Guild ads on pages 18, 19, and 256.

I am proud to be associated with the Graphic Artists Guild's DIRECTORY OF ILLUSTRATION, and trust that everyone who looks through these pages will appreciate the talent and hard work that goes into being a professional commercial illustrator.

Legal Guide for the Visual Artist by Tad Crawford

Allworth Press, New York 1990

GLEN ROBERT SERBIN

Publisher

ARTICLES OF THE CODE OF FAIR PRACTICE

This code provides the graphic communications industry with an accepted standard of ethics and professional conduct. It presents guidelines for the voluntary conduct of persons in the industry, which may be modified by written agreement between the parties.

ARTICLE 1. Negotiations between an artist* or the artist's representative and a client should be conducted only through an authorized buyer.

ARTICLE 2. Orders or agreements between an artist or artist's representative and buyer should be in writing and shall include the specific rights which are being transferred, the specific fee arrangement agreed to by the parties, delivery date, and a summarized description of the work.

ARTICLE 3. All changes or additions not due to the fault of the artist or artist's representative should be billed to the buyer as an additional and separate charge.

ARTICLE 4. There should be no charges to the buyer for revisions or retakes made necessary by errors on the part of the artist or the artist's representative.

ARTICLE 5. If work commissioned by a buyer is postponed or cancelled, a "kill-fee" should be negotiated based on time allotted, effort expended, and expenses incurred.

ARTICLE 6. Completed work shall be paid for in full and the artwork shall be returned promptly to the artist.

ARTICLE 7. Alterations shall not be made without consulting the artist. Where alterations or retakes are necessary, the artist shall be given the opportunity of making such changes.

ARTICLE 8. The artist shall notify the buyer of any anticipated delay in delivery. Should the artist fail to keep the contract through unreasonable delay or non-conformance with agreed specifications, it will be considered a breach of contract by the artist.

ARTICLE 9. Asking an artist to work on speculation is not deemed professionally reasonable because of its potentially exploitative nature.

ARTICLE 10. There shall be no undisclosed rebates, discounts, gifts, or bonuses requested by or given to buyers by the artist or representative.

ARTICLE 11. Artwork and copyright ownership are vested in the hands of the artist.

ARTICLE 12. Original artwork remains the property of the artist unless it is specifically purchased. It is distinct from the purchase of any reproduction rights.* *All transactions shall be in writing.

ARTICLE 13. In case of copyright transfers, only specified rights are transferred. All unspecified rights remain vested with the artist. **All transactions shall be in writing.

ARTICLE 14. Commissioned artwork is not to be considered as "work for hire."

ARTICLE 15. When the price of work is based on limited use and later such work is used more extensively, the artist shall receive additional payment.

ARTICLE 16. If exploratory work, comprehensives, or preliminary photographs are bought from an artist with the intention or possibility that another artist will be assigned to do the finished work, this shall be in writing at the time of placing the order.

ARTICLE 18. If no transfer of copyright ownership* has been executed, the publisher of any reproduction of artwork shall publish the artist's copyright notice if the artist so requests at the time of agreement.

ARTICLE 19. The right to remove the artist's name on published artwork is subject to agreement between artist and buyer.

ARTICLE 20. There shall be no plagiarism of any artwork.

ARTICLE 21. If an artist is specifically requested to produce any artwork during unreasonable working hours, fair additional remuneration shall be paid.

ARTICLE 22. All artwork or photography submitted as samples to a buyer should bear the name of the artist or artists responsible for the work. An artist shall not claim authorship of another's work.

ARTICLE 23. All companies and their employees who receive artist portfolios, samples, etc. shall be responsible for the return of the portfolio to the artist in the same condition as received.

ARTICLE 24. An artist entering into an agreement with a representative, studio, or production company for an exclusive representation shall not accept an order from nor permit work to be shown by any other representative or studio. Any agreement which is not intended to be exclusive should set forth the exact restrictions agreed upon between the parties.

ARTICLE 25. No representative should continue to show an artist's samples after the termination of an association.

ARTICLE 26. After termination of an association between artist and representative, the representative should be entitled to a commission for a period of six months on accounts which the representative has secured, unless otherwise specified by contract.

ARTICLE 27. Examples of an artist's work furnished to a representative or submitted to a prospective buyer shall remain the property of the artist, should not be duplicated without the artist's consent, and shall be returned promptly to the artist in good condition.

ARTICLE 28. Contests for commercial purposes are not deemed professionally reasonable because of their potentially speculative and exploitative character.

ARTICLE 29. Interpretation of the Code for the purposes of mediation and arbitration shall be in the hands of the Joint Ethics Committee and is subject to changes and additions at the discretion of the parent organizations through their appointed representatives on the Committee.

Submitting to mediation and arbitration under the auspices of the Joint Ethics Committee is voluntary and requires the consent of all parties to the dispute.

LIST OF ARTISTS AND REPRESENTATIVES

A

A.M. STUDIOS	153-157
ABRAMOWITZ FINE ARTS, INC.	222-223
ALLEN, TERRY	232
AMOROSI, TERESA	191
AMOROSI, THOMAS	191
ANDELIN, DOUGLAS	80
ANGLE, SCOTT	201
ANSELY, FRANK	164

B

BAIER, MATT	229
BARBIER, SUZETTE	155
BARRERA, POLO	253
BARRETT, JACK	133
BARUFFI, ANDREA	179
BASEMAN, GARY	54-55
BEGO, DOLORES	72
BIANCO, PETER	115
BILLOUT, GUY	197
BLACKWELL, PATRICK	253
BLANK, JERRY RUSSELL	174-175
BODDY, JOE	91
BOLTON, ANDREA	110
BON DURANT, STEVE	160-161
BONO, PETER	250
BOWLES, BRUCE	198
BRALDS, BRALDT	46-47
BROWN, MARK KINGSLEY	82
BROWN, SUE ELLEN	217
BRUGGER, BOB	238

BURGIO, TRISH	64-65
BYER, LOU	193

C

CAMARENA, MIGUEL	105
CAPPARELLI, TONY	252
CARBONE, LOUIS	122
CARLSON, FREDERICK	134
CARROZZA, CYNTHIA	116
CARSON, JIM	194
CATALANO, SAL	148
CATHCART, MARILYN	154
CHID	125
CHING, DARREN	186
CLEGG, DAVID	221
COFFELT, KEN	84-85
COHEN, SHAY	251
COLE, DICK	169
CONSOLE, JR., CARMEN	90
CRAFT, KINUKO	22-23
CROMB, BOB	195

D

DAWSON, JOHN	24-25
DEETER, CATHERINE	26-27
DEGROAT, DIANE	183
DELUZ, TONY	226
DEPALMA, MARY NEWELL	156
DETRICH, SUSAN	150
DIEFENDORF, CATHY	180
DOGUE, MAURICE	173
DOUGHTY, ROBERT	98

DUDASH, MICHAEL	60
DUFOUR LOVE, JUDITH	153
DUGAN, BRIAN	71
DURFEE, THOMAS	190

E

ENOS, RANDALL	70
ERICKSON, KERNE	108
EVANS, GLEN	99

F

FARACLAS JENNISON, ANDREA	145
FERSTER, GARY	132
FLEMING, DEAN	159
FOSTER, MATT	248-249
FOWLER, ERIC	95
FRALEY, KIM	101
FREEMAN, LAURA	218

G

GAETANO, NICK	237
GALLAGHER, MATTHEW	114
GANTON, CHRISTOPHER	61
GAY, PATTI	224
GENZO, JOHN PAUL	119
GESER, GRETCHEN	122
GIBBONS, BILL	165
GIUSTI, ROBERT	36-37
GLAZER, ART	178
GOLDSTEIN, GWEN	180-181
GOLDSTROM, ROBERT	49

ARTISTS

GORMAN, STAN	107	JOHNSON, STEPHEN	62-63	MASCIOVECCHIO, MARIE	254
GRANING, KEN	87	JOLY, DAVE	184	McDANIEL, JERRY	73
GRAY, STEVE	172	JONES, CATHERINE	176	McENTIRE, LARRY	32-33
GREENSTEIN, SUSAN	129	JONES, DANIELLE	234-235	McGURL, MICHAEL	151
GREGORY, ERRICO	138	JUHASZ, VICTOR	40-41	McLEAN, WILSON	66-67
GREGORY, LANE	181	JUSKO, JOE	219	MEEHAN, KEITH	161
GRIEN, ANITA	72-73	JUST, HAL	73	MEIER, DAVID SCOTT	103

H

K

				MELLET-BERRY, FANNY	72
HAMILL, PAUL	209	KANE, JOHN	245	M'GUINNESS, JIM	89
HARRELSON, PAMELA	92	KELENY, EARL	30-31	MIDDENDORF, FRANCES	137
HARRINGTON, GLENN	192	KELLEY, PATRICK	188	MILLER, MARCIA	88
HARRISON, HUGH	139	KLEIN, RENEE	233	MINOR, WENDELL	50-51
HEALY, DEBORAH	58-59			MINOT, KAREN	212
HESS, MARK	42-43			MONTGOMERY, M. K.	112
HESS, RICHARD	35			MORECRAFT, RON	152

L

				MORRISON, CATHY	244
HILL, KENNIE	193	L.A. SOCIETY OF ILLUSTRATORS	97-112	MORRISON, DON	72
HIROKO	167	LATTO, SOPHIA	127		
HOGAN, SHANNON	106	LAUTENSLAGER, PETER	177		
HOKANSON, LARS	28-29	LAW, POLLY	202-203		

N

HOLDER, JIMMY	182	LEE, JARED	83	MILTON NEWBORN & ASSOCIATES,	35-53
HOVLAND, GARY	185	LEECH, DOROTHY	126	NOISET, MICHELE	76
HOWARD, JOHN	48	LEVINSON, DAVID	94		
HOWELL, VAN	246	LEVY LIBERMAN, JONI	155		

O

HUFFMAN, TOM	135	LEWIS, TIM	131	O'KEEFE YOUNG, MARY	199
		LUNDGREN, TIMOTHY	220		

I

P

		LYTLE, JOHN	210		
ICON GRAPHICS	160-161			PEDERSEN, JUDY	56-57

M

				PIETROBONO, JANET	189

J

		MACEREN, JUDE	113	POSEY, PAM	100
JOHNSON, JULIE	73	MACHAT, MIKE	104	PRENTICE, LYNNE	215
JOHNSON, LONNI SUE	117	MARTINOT, CLAUDE	74		

ARTISTS

PRZEWODEK, CAMILLE	20	SKEEN, KEITH	200	TREATNER, MERYL	170-171
PUNCHATZ, DON	230	SMITH, JEFFREY	242-243	TYLER, CRAIG	214
		SMITH, THERESA	176		
R		SMITH, WILLIAM	241		
RAGLAND, GREG	93	SMYTH, RICHARD	163	**U**	
RAINOCK, NORMAN	187	SOCIETY OF ILLUSTRATION/L.A.	97		
RAMAGE, ALFRED	124	SOKOLOWSKI, TED	247	UNGER, JUDY	102
RAMSEY, CARL	78-79	SPELLMAN, SUSAN	180	URBANOVIC, JACKIE	77
RAPP, INC., GERALD & CULLEN	20, 21	SPELMAN, STEVE	21		
REINGOLD, ALAN	72	SPIECE, JIM	231	**V**	
RHODES, BARBARA	162	STANFILL, MIKE	240		
RIEDY, MARK	239	STEDMAN, EMILY	86	VELTFORT, ANNA	142
RIXFORD, ELLEN	118	STUBBS, ELIZABETH	156	VINCENT, BENJAMIN	240
ROMER, DAN	158	SUTTON, JUDITH	146-147	VON MORISSE, ANDRE	109
ROSENTHAL, MARC	206	SUVIT-YASIRI, SARN	75		
ROSS, MARY	205	SWAN, SUSAN	121	**W**	
ROUNDTREE, DEBORAH	21	SWANSON, JAMES	34		
RUFFINS, REYNOLD	52-53	SWEARINGEN, KAREN MEYER	208	WALDMAN, BRYNA	236
RUSSELL, BILL	196	SYMINGTON, GARY	143	WALTER, NANCY LEE	81
		SYSKA, RICHARD	228	WEILAND, GARISON	130
S				WHITESIDES, KIM	68-69
		T		WILCOX, DAVID	38-39
SALVATORE, ROSEMARY	207			WILLIAMS, TOBY	154
SAYAD, MARDUK	166	TABACK, SIMMS	44-45	WINN-LEDERER, ILENE	136
SCALI, SAM	96	TALCOTT, JULIA	157		
SCHROEDER, MARK	211	TALEPOROS, PLATO	144	**Y**	
SCHWARTZ, JUDITH	213	TAYLOR, C. WINSTON	111		
SCHWEIGERT, CAROL	126	THELEN, MARY	225	YULE, SUSAN	123
SEAVER, JEFF	140	THOMAS, ROD	216		
SEIGEL, FRAN	22-33	THORNTON, BLAKE	149	**Z**	
SHACHAT, ANDREW	168	TORRES, LEYLA	204		
SIERRA, DOROTHEA	141	TORRISI, GARY	181	ZWARENSTEIN, ALEX	73
SILVESTRI, STEPHEN	227				

EASY ACCESS INDEX

The following listings reflect the subjects shown on the artists' pages, and do not necessarily demonstrate the full range of their skills.

ADVENTURE

ABRAMOWITZ FINE ARTS, INC.	222-223
BLACKWELL, PATRICK	253
BODDY, JOE	91
BRALDS, BRALDT	46-47
CRAFT, KINUKO	22-23
DAWSON, JOHN	24-25
DEETER, CATHERINE	26-27
DIEFENDORF, CATHY	180
FERSTER, GARY	132
GAETANO, NICK	237
GOLDSTEIN, GWEN	180-181
GREGORY, LANE	181
HESS, RICHARD	35
HESS, MARK	42-43
HOKANSON, LARS	28-29
KELENY, EARL	30-31
LEVY LIBERMAN, JONI	155
LYTLE, JOHN	210
MACEREN, JUDE	113
McENTIRE, LARRY	32-33
MINOR, WENDELL	50-51
PUNCHATZ, DON	230
SEIGEL, FRANK	22-33
SYSKA, RICHARD	228
TORRISI, GARY	181
WALDMAN, BRYNA	236
WHITESIDES, KIM	68-69

ANIMALS

ABRAMOWITZ FINE ARTS, INC.	222-223
AMOROSI, THOMAS	191
AMOROSI, TERESA	191
ANDELIN, DOUGLAS	80
BARBIER, SUZETTE	155
BLACKWELL, PATRICK	253
BODDY, JOE	91
BOLTON, ANDREA	110

BRALDS, BRALDT	46-47
BROWN, SUE ELLEN	217
CARSON, JIM	194
CATALANO, SAL	148
CATHCART, MARILYN	154
CHID	125
CLEGG, DAVID	221
COHEN, SHAY	251
CRAFT, KINUKO	22-23
CROMB, BOB	195
DAWSON, JOHN	24-25
DEETER, CATHERINE	26-27
DEGROAT, DIANE	183
DETRICH, SUSAN	150
DIEFENDORF, CATHY	180
DUDASH, MICHAEL	60
DUFOUR LOVE, JUDITH	153
ENOS, RANDALL	70
ERICKSON, KERNE	108
FERSTER, GARY	132
FRALEY, KIM	101
GAETANO, NICK	237
GAY, PATTI	224
GENZO, JOHN PAUL	119
GIUSTI, ROBERT	36-37
GOLDSTEIN, GWEN	180-181
GOLDSTROM, ROBERT	49
GREGORY, LANE	181
HAMILL, PAUL	209
HARRELSON, PAMELA	92
HESS, RICHARD	35
HESS, MARK	42-43
HIROKO	167
HOLDER, JIMMY	182
HOWELL, VAN	246
JONES, DANIELLE	234-235
KANE, JOHN	245
LEE, JARED	83
LEECH, DOROTHY	126
LUNDGREN, TIMOTHY	220
LYTLE, JOHN	210
MACEREN, JUDE	113
MARTINOT, CLAUDE	74
McENTIRE, LARRY	32-33
McLEAN, WILSON	66-67
M'GUINNESS, JIM	89

MINOR, WENDELL	50-51
NEWELL DEPALMA, MARY	156
NOISET, MICHELE	76
PEDERSEN, JUDY	56-57
POSEY, PAM	100
PRENTICE, LYNNE	215
PUNCHATZ, DON	230
RAMAGE, ALFRED	124
ROSS, MARY	205
RUFFINS, REYNOLD	52-53
SCALI, SAM	96
SCHWARTZ, JUDITH	213
SEAVER, JEFF	140
SEIGEL, FRAN	22-33
SIERRA, DOROTHEA	141
SMITH, JEFFREY	242-243
SUTTON, JUDITH	146-147
SWAN, SUSAN	121
SYSKA, RICHARD	228
TABACK, SIMMS	44-45
THOMAS, ROD	216
TORRES, LEYLA	204
TORRISI, GARY	181
TREATNER, MERYL	170-171
VINCENT, BENJAMIN	240
WALDMAN, BRYNA	236
WALTER, NANCY LEE	81
WILCOX, DAVID	38-39
WILLIAMS, TOBY	154
WINN-LEDERER, ILENE	136

ANIMATION

BLACKWELL, PATRICK	253
DIEFENDORF, CATHY	180
DURFEE, THOMAS	190
GREGORY, LANE	181
HOKANSON, LARS	28-29
JOHNSON, LONNI SUE	117
JONES, DANIELLE	234-235
LEE, JARED	83
RUFFINS, REYNOLD	52-53
TABACK, SIMMS	44-45
TORRISI, GARY	181

ARCHITECTURAL

ANDELIN, DOUGLAS	80
BILLOUT, GUY	197
CARROZZA, CYNTHIA	116
COLE, DICK	169
CONSOLE, JR., CARMEN	90
DELUZ, TONY	226
DETRICH, SUSAN	150
DIEFENDORF, CATHY	180
DUDASH, MICHAEL	60
GOLDSTEIN, GWEN	180-181
GOLDSTROM, ROBERT	49
GREGORY, LANE	181
HESS, RICHARD	35
HESS, MARK	42-43
HOWARD, JOHN	48
JUHASZ, VICTOR	40-41
KANE, JOHN	245
MARTINOT, CLAUDE	74
McLEAN, WILSON	66-67
M'GUINESS, JIM	89
MORECRAFT, RON	152
PEDERSEN, JUDY	56-57
PRZEWODEK, CAMILLE	20
PUNCHATZ, DON	230
RIXFORD, ELLEN	118
SCHROEDER, MARK	211
SCHWARTZ, JUDITH	213
SIERRA, DOROTHEA	141
SWEARINGEN, KAREN MEYER	208
TORRISI, GARY	181
WHITESIDES, KIM	68-69
WILCOX, DAVID	38-39
YULE, SUSAN	123

BOOK

ABRAMOWITZ FINE ARTS, INC.	222-223
AMOROSI, THOMAS	191
AMOROSI, TERESA	191
ANDELIN, DOUGLAS	80
BARBIER, SUZETTE	155
BASEMAN, GARY	54-55
BODDY, JOE	91
BOWLES, BRUCE	198

EASY ACCESS INDEX

BRALDS, BRALDT 46-47
BURGIO, TRISH 64-65
CARBONE, LOUIS 122
CARLSON, FREDERICK 134
CARROZZA, CYNTHIA 116
CATALANO, SAL 148
CATHCART, MARILYN 154
CHING, DARREN 186
CRAFT, KINUKO 22-23
DAWSON, JOHN 24-25
DEETER, CATHERINE 26-27
DELUZ, TONY 226
DETRICH, SUSAN 150
DIEFENDORF, CATHY 180
DUDASH, MICAHEL 60
DUFOUR LOVE, JUDITH 153
ENOS, RANDALL 70
FARACLAS JENNISON, ANDREA 145
FERSTER, GARY 132
FLEMING, DEAN 159
FOWLER, ERIC 95
FRALEY, KIM 101
FREEMAN, LAURA 218
GAETANO, NICK 237
GANTON, CHRISTOPHER 61
GENZO, JOHN PAUL 119
GESER, GRETCHEN 122
GIBBONS, BILL 165
GIUSTI, ROBERT 36-37
GOLDSTEIN, GWEN 180-181
GOLDSTROM, ROBERT 49
GRANING, KEN 87
GREENSTEIN, SUSAN 129
GREGORY, LANE 181
HAMILL, PAUL 209
HARRELSON, PAMELA 92
HARRISON, HUGH 139
HEALY, DEBORAH 58-59
HESS, RICHARD 35
HESS, MARK 42-43
HIROKO 167
HOGAN, SHANNON 106
HOKANSON, LARS 28-29
HOWARD, JOHN 48
HOWELL, VAN 246
JOHNSON, LONNI SUE 117

JOHNSON, STEPHEN 62-63
JONES, CATHERINE 176
JONES, DANIELLE 234-235
JUHASZ, VICTOR 40-41
KELENY, EARL 30-31
KELLEY, PATRICK 188
LATTO, SOPHIA 127
LEE, JARED 83
LEECH, DOROTHY 126
LEVY LIBERMAN, JONI 155
LYTLE, JOHN 210
MACEREN, JUDE 113
MASCIOVECCHIO, MARIE 254
McDANIEL, JERRY 73
McENTIRE, LARRY 32-33
McLEAN, WILSON 66-67
MEIER, DAVID SCOTT 103
MELLET-BERRY, FANNY 72
M'GUINNESS, JIM 89
MIDDENDORF, FRANCES 137
MILLER, MARCIA 88
MINOR, WENDELL 50-51
MONTGOMERY, M.K. 112
MORECRAFT, RON 152
MORRISON, CATHY 244
NEWELL DEPALMA, MARY 156
NOISET, MICHELE 76
O'KEEFE YOUNG, MARY 199
PEDERSEN, JUDY 56-57
POSEY, PAM 100
PRENTICE, LYNNE 215
PUNCHATZ, DON 230
RAGLAND, GREG 93
RAMAGE, ALFRED 124
REINGOLD, ALAN 72
RHODES, BARBARA 162
RUSSELL, BILL 196
SCHWARTZ, JUDITH 213
SCHWEIGERT, CAROL 120
SEIGEL, FRAN 22-33
SHACHAT, ANDREW 168
SIERRA, DOROTHEA 141
SKEEN, KEITH 200
SMITH, THERESA 176
SOKOLOWSKI, TED 247
STEDMAN, EMILY 86

SUTTON, JUDITH 146-147
SWAN, SUSAN 121
SWANSON, JAMES 34
SWEARINGEN, KAREN MEYER 208
SYMINGTON, GARY 143
SYSKA, RICHARD 228
THELEN, MARY 225
THOMAS, ROD 216
TORRISI, GARY 181
TREATNER, MERYL 170-171
URBANOVIC, JACKIE 77
VELTFORT, ANNA 142
VON MORISSE, ANDRE 109
WALDMAN, BRYNA 236
WALTER, NANCY LEE 81
WEILAND, GARISON 130
WILCOX, DAVID 38-39
WILLIAMS, TOBY 154
WINN-LEDERER, ILENE 136

CARICATURE

ANDELIN, DOUGLAS 80
ANGLE, SCOTT 201
BAIER, MATT 229
BASEMAN, GARY 54-55
BLACKWELL, PATRICK 253
BONO, PETER 250
CHID 125
CLEGG, DAVID 221
DIEFENDORF, CATHY 180
DOUGHTY, ROBERT 98
ENOS, RANDALL 70
EVANS, GLEN 99
GANTON, CHRISTOPHER 61
GOLDSTEIN, GWEN 180-181
GREGORY, LANE 181
HEALY, DEBORAH 58-59
HOLDER, JIMMY 182
HOWELL, VAN 246
JONES, DANIELLE 234-235
JUHASZ, VICTOR 40-41
JUST, HAL 73
KELLEY, PATRICK 188
MACEREN, JUDE 113
MASCIOVECCHIO, MARIE 254

M'GUINNESS, JIM 89
NOISET, MICHELE 76
PUNCHATZ, DON 230
RAMAGE, ALFRED 124
ROSS, MARY 205
SYSKA, RICHARD 228
THOMAS, ROD 216
TORRISI, GARY 181
TREATNER, MERYL 170-171
VINCENT, BENJAMIN 240
WINN-LEDERER, ILENE 136

CHARTS & MAPS

AMOROSI, THOMAS 191
AMOROSI, TERESA 191
ANDELIN, DOUGLAS 80
BEGO, DOLORES 72
DIEFENDORF, CATHY 180
FERSTER, GARY 132
GOLDSTEIN, GWEN 180-181
GREENSTEIN, SUSAN 129
GREGORY, LANE 181
HOWELL, VAN 246
LEVY LIBERMAN, JONI 155
MARTINOT, CLAUDE 74
MINOT, KAREN 212
PUNCHATZ, DON 230
SYSKA, RICHARD 228
TORRISI, GARY 181

CHILDREN

ABRAMOWITZ FINE ARTS, INC. 222-223
AMOROSI, THOMAS 191
AMOROSI, TERESA 191
BASEMAN, GARY 54-55
BLACKWELL, PATRICK 253
BODDY, JOE 91
BOLTON, ANDREA 110
BOWLES, BRUCE 198
CARSON, JIM 194
CATALANO, SAL 148
CHID 125
CLEGG, DAVID 221
CRAFT, KINUKO 22-23

EASY ACCESS INDEX

DEETER, CATHERINE   26-27
DEGROAT, DIANE   183
DELUZ, TONY   226
DIEFENDORF, CATHY   180
DOUGHTY, ROBERT   98
DUFOUR LOVE, JUDITH   153
DURFEE, THOMAS   190
FARACLAS JENNISON, ANDREA 145
GAY, PATTI   224
GOLDSTEIN, GWEN   180-181
GREGORY, LANE   181
HAMILL, PAUL   209
HARRELSON, PAMELA   92
HEALY, DEBORAH   58-59
HOGAN, SHANNON   106
HOLDER, JIMMY   182
JONES, DANIELLE   234-235
KELLEY, PATRICK   188
LATTO, SOPHIA   127
LAW, POLLY   202-203
LEE, JARED   83
LEECH, DOROTHY   126
LEVY LIBERMAN, JONI   155
LYTLE, JOHN   210
MARTINOT, CLAUDE   74
McENTIRE, LARRY   32-33
M'GUINNESS, JIM   89
MILLER, MARCIA   88
MORRISON, CATHY   244
NEWELL DEPALMA, MARY   156
NOISET, MICHELE   76
O'KEEFE YOUNG, MARY   199
PEDERSEN, JUDY   56-57
PIETROBONO, JANET   189
PRZEWODEK, CAMILLE   20
RAMAGE, ALFRED   124
ROSS, MARY   205
RUFFINS, REYNOLD   52-53
SALVATORE, ROSEMARY   207
SEIGEL, FRAN   22-33
SIERRA, DOROTHEA   141
SPELMAN, STEVE   21
STEDMAN, EMILY   86
SUTTON, JUDITH   146-147
SWEARINGEN, KAREN MEYER   208
SYSKA, RICHARD   228

TABACK, SIMMS   44-45
THELEN, MARY   225
TORRISI, GARY   181
TREATNER, MERYL   170-171
WALDMAN, BRYNA   236
WILLIAMS, TOBY   154
WINN-LEDERER, ILENE   136
ZWARENSTEIN, ALEX   73

CHILDREN'S BOOKS & PRODUCTS

ABRAMOWITZ FINE ARTS, INC. 222-223
AMOROSI, THOMAS   191
AMOROSI, TERESA   191
BARBIER, SUZETTE   155
BASEMAN, GARY   54-55
BODDY, JOE   91
BON DURANT, STEVE   160-161
BROWN, SUE ELLEN   217
BRUGGER, BOB   238
CARROZZA, CYNTHIA   116
CARSON, JIM   194
CHID   125
CRAFT, KINUKO   22-23
DAWSON, JOHN   24-25
DEETER, CATHERINE   26-27
DIEFENDORF, CATHY   180
DUFOUR LOVE, JUDITH   153
DURFEE, THOMAS   190
ENOS, RANDALL   70
FARACLAS JENNISON, ANDREA 145
FREEMAN, LAURA   218
GAY, PATTI   224
GESER, GRETCHEN   122
GOLDSTEIN, GWEN   180-181
GREENSTEIN, SUSAN   129
GREGORY, LANE   181
HAMILL, PAUL   209
HARRELSON, PAMELA   92
HEALY, DEBORAH   58-59
HOGAN, SHANNON   106
HOKANSON, LARS   28-29
HOLDER, JIMMY   182

HUFFMAN, TOM   135
ICON GRAPHICS   160-161
JOHNSON, LONNI SUE   117
JOLY, DAVE   184
JONES, CATHERINE   176
JONES, DANIELLE   234-235
KELLEY, PATRICK   188
LATTO, SOPHIA   127
LEE, JARED   83
LEECH, DOROTHY   126
LEVY LIBERMAN, JONI   155
MACEREN, JUDE   113
McENTIRE, LARRY   32-33
MEEHAN, KEITH   161
MELLET-BERRY, FANNY   72
M'GUINNESS, JIM   89
MILLER, MARCIA   88
MORECRAFT, RON   152
MORRISON, CATHY   244
NEWELL DEPALMA, MARY   156
NOISET, MICHELE   76
O'KEEFE YOUNG, MARY   199
PEDERSEN, JUDY   56-57
PIETROBONO, JANET   189
ROSS, MARY   205
RUFFINS, REYNOLD   52-53
SCALI, SAM   96
SEAVER, JEFF   140
SEIGEL, FRAN   22-33
SHACHAT, ANDREW   168
SIERRA, DOROTHEA   141
SMITH, THERESA   176
STEDMAN, EMILY   86
SUTTON, JUDITH   146-147
SWAN, SUSAN   121
SWEARINGEN, KAREN MEYER   208
SYSKA, RICHARD   228
TABACK, SIMMS   44-45
THELEN, MARY   225
THOMAS, ROD   216
TORRES, LEYLA   204
TORRISI, GARY   181
TREATNER, MERYL   170-171
TYLER, CRAIG   214
URBANOVIC, JACKIE   77
VELTFORT, ANNA   142

VINCENT, BENJAMIN   240
WALDMAN, BRYNA   236
WALTER, NANCY LEE   81
WILLIAMS, TOBY   154
WINN-LEDERER, ILENE   136

COLLAGE

ANDELIN, DOUGLAS   80
BLACKWELL, PATRICK   253
CATALANO, SAL   148
DIEFENDORF, CATHY   180
FERSTER, GARY   132
GOLDSTEIN, GWEN   180-181
GREGORY, LANE   181
HARRELSON, PAMELA   92
MORECRAFT, RON   152
ROMER, DAN   158
SALVATORE, ROSEMARY   207
SCHWARTZ, JUDITH   213
SPELMAN, STEVE   21
THELEN, MARY   225
TORRISI, GARY   181

FASHION & COSMETICS

ABRAMOWITZ FINE ARTS, INC. 222-223
BLACKWELL, PATRICK   253
BOLTON, ANDREA   110
BURGIO, TRISH   64-65
DEETER, CATHERINE   26-27
DIEFENDORF, CATHY   180
GOLDSTEIN, GWEN   180-181
GREGORY, LANE   181
HARRELSON, PAMELA   92
HEALY, DEBORAH   58-59
HOGAN, SHANNON   106
JOHNSON, JULIE   73
JONES, CATHERINE   176
LEVY LIBERMAN, JONI   155
MACEREN, JUDE   113
MORECRAFT, RON   152
MORRISON, DON   72
O'KEEFE YOUNG, MARY   199

EASY ACCESS INDEX

PRZEWODEK, CAMILLE	20
RHODES, BARBARA	162
ROUNDTREE, DEBORAH	21
SMITH, THERESA	176
SPELMAN, STEVE	21
SYSKA, RICHARD	228
TORRISI, GARY	181
TREATNER, MERYL	170-171
WALDMAN, BRYNA	236

FOOD

ANDELIN, DOUGLAS	80
BARBIER, SUZANNE	155
BLACKWELL, PATRICK	253
CARBONE, LOUIS	122
CARROZZA, CYNTHIA	116
COHEN, SHAY	251
COLE, DICK	169
DEETER, CATHERINE	26-27
DIEFENDORF, CATHY	180
DUGAN, BRIAN	71
FARACLAS JENNISON, ANDREA	145
FERSTER, GARY	132
FLEMING, DEAN	159
FOSTER, MATT	248-249
GENZO, JOHN PAUL	119
GOLDSTEIN, GWEN	180-181
GREENSTEIN, SUSAN	129
GREGORY, LANE	181
HAMILL, PAUL	209
HARRELSON, PAMELA	92
HEALY, DEBORAH	58-59
HOGAN, SHANNON	106
HOKANSON, LARS	28-29
JOHNSON, LONNI SUE	117
JONES, CATHERINE	176
JUST, HAL	73
KANE, JOHN	245
LATTO, SOPHIA	127
LAW, POLLY	202-203
LEECH, DOROTHY	126
LEVY LIBERMAN, JONI	155
McENTIRE, LARRY	32-33
PEDERSEN, JUDY	56-57
PRENTICE, LYNNE	215

PRZEWODEK, CAMILLE	20
PUNCHATZ, DON	230
RAMAGE, ALFRED	124
RHODES, BARBARA	162
ROUNDTREE, DEBORAH	21
RUSSELL, BILL	196
SIERRA, DOROTHEA	141
SMITH, THERESA	176
SWEARINGEN, KAREN MEYER	208
SYMINGTON, GARY	143
SYSKA, RICHARD	228
TORRES, LEYLA	204
TORRISI, GARY	181
UNGER, JUDY	102
WINN-LEDERER, ILENE	136

GRAPHIC DESIGN & LETTERING

ANDELIN, DOUGLAS	80
BARRETT, JACK	133
BON DURANT, STEVE	160-161
BYER, LOU	193
COHEN, SHAY	251
CONSOLE, JR., CARMEN	90
DIEFENDORF, CATHY	180
DUGAN, BRIAN	71
ERICKSON, KERNE	108
EVANS, GLEN	99
FERSTER, GARY	132
GAETANO, NICK	237
GALLAGHER, MATTHEW	146
GOLDSTEIN, GWEN	180-181
GREGORY, ERRICO	138
GREGORY, LANE	181
HARRELSON, PAMELA	92
HILL, KENNIE	193
HOKANSON, LARS	28-29
ICON GRAPHICS	160-161
JUST, HAL	73
LEECH, DOROTHY	126
McDANIEL, JERRY	73
MEEHAN, KEITH	161
MONTGOMERY, M.K.	112

PUNCHATZ, DON	230
SCHWARTZ, JUDITH	213
SILVESTRI, STEPHEN	227
SPIECE, JIM	231
STANFILL, MIKE	240
SYSKA, RICHARD	228
TALCOTT, JULIA	157
TAYLOR, C. WINSTON	111
THORNTON, BLAKE	149
TORRISI, GARY	181
WHITESIDES, KIM	68-69
WINN-LEDERER, ILENE	136

HUMOR

ANDELIN, DOUGLAS	80
ANGLE, SCOTT	201
ANSELY, FRANK	164
BARBIER, SUZETTE	155
BARUFFI, ANDREA	179
BASEMAN, GARY	54-55
BIANCO, PETER	115
BLACKWELL, PATRICK	253
BODDY, JOE	91
BONO, PETER	250
BOWLES, BRUCE	198
BROWN, MARK KINGSLEY	82
BRUGGER, BOB	238
BYER, LOU	193
CARBONE, LOUIS	122
CARSON, JIM	194
CHID	125
CLEGG, DAVID	221
CROMB, BOB	195
DAWSON, JOHN	24-25
DIEFENDORF, CATHY	180
DUFOUR LOVE, JUDITH	153
DURFEE, THOMAS	190
ENOS, RANDALL	70
EVANS, GLEN	99
FREEMAN, LAURA	218
GANTON, CHRISTOPHER	61
GLAZER, ART	178
GOLDSTEIN, GWEN	180-181
GORMAN, STAN	107
GRAY, STEVE	172

GREGORY, LANE	181
HARRELSON, PAMELA	92
HESS, MARK	42-43
HILL, KENNIE	193
HOKANSON, LARS	28-29
HOLDER, JIMMY	182
HOVLAND, GARY	185
HOWARD, JOHN	48
HOWELL, VAN	246
HUFFMAN, TOM	135
JOHNSON, LONNI SUE	117
JOLY, DAVE	184
JONES, CATHERINE	176
JONES, DANIELLE	234-235
JUHASZ, VICTOR	40-41
JUST, HAL	73
KANE, JOHN	245
KELLEY, PATRICK	188
LEE, JARED	83
MARTINOT, CLAUDE	74
MASCIOVECCHIO, MARIE	254
McENTIRE, LARRY	32-33
McGURL, MICHAEL	151
MELLET-BERRY, FANNY	72
M'GUINNESS, JIM	89
MORRISON, CATHY	244
NOISET, MICHELE	76
RAINOCK, NORMAN	187
RAMAGE, ALFRED	124
RIXFORD, ELLEN	118
ROMER, DAN	158
ROSENTHAL, MARC	206
ROSS, MARY	205
RUFFINS, REYNOLD	52-53
SAYAD, MARDUK	166
SEAVER, JEFF	140
SHACHAT, ANDREW	168
SKEEN, KEITH	200
SMITH, THERESA	176
STANFILL, MIKE	240
SWAN, SUSAN	121
SYSKA, RICHARD	228
TABACK, SIMMS	44-45
TALCOTT, JULIA	157
TALEPOROS, PLATO	144
THELEN, MARY	225

EASY ACCESS INDEX

THOMAS, ROD 216
TORRISI, GARY 181
TYLER, CRAIG 214
URBANOVIC, JACKIE 77
VELTFORT, ANNA 142
VINCENT, BENJAMIN 240
WALTER, NANCY LEE 81
WEILAND, GARISON 130
WHITESIDES, KIM 68-69
WILLIAMS, TOBY 154
WINN-LEDERER, ILENE 136
YULE, SUSAN 123
ZWARENSTEIN, ALEX 73

LANDSCAPE

ABRAMOWITZ FINE ARTS, INC. 222-223
AMOROSI, THOMAS 191
AMOROSI, TERESA 191
BARBIER, SUZETTE 155
BLACKWELL, PATRICK 253
BRALDS, BRALDT 46-47
CARLSON, FREDERICK 134
CARROZZA, CYNTHIA 116
CATHCART, MARILYN 154
COLE, DICK 169
CRAFT, KINUKO 22-23
DEETER, CATHERINE 26-27
DELUZ, TONY 226
DETRICH, SUSAN 150
DIEFENDORF, CATHY 180
DUDASH, MICHAEL 60
FERSTER, GARY 132
GAY, PATTI 224
GIUSTI, ROBERT 36-37
GOLDSTEIN, GWEN 180-181
GOLDSTROM, ROBERT 49
GRANING, KEN 87
GREENSTEIN, SUSAN 129
GREGORY, LANE 181
HEALY, DEBORAH 58-59
HESS, RICHARD 35
HIROKO 167
HOKANSON, LARS 28-29
HOWARD, JOHN 48
JOHNSON, LONNI SUE 117

JONES, CATHERINE 176
JUHASZ, VICTOR 40-41
KANE, JOHN 245
KELENY, EARL 30-31
LATTO, SOPHIA 127
LUNDGREN, TIMOTHY 220
LYTLE, JOHN 210
McENTIRE, LARRY 32-33
McLEAN, WILSON 66-67
M'GUINNESS, JIM 89
MILLER, MARCIA 88
MINOR, WENDELL 50-51
MINOT, KAREN 212
MORECRAFT, RON 152
O'KEEFE YOUNG, MARY 199
PEDERSEN, JUDY 56-57
PIETROBONO, JANET 189
PRZEWODEK, CAMILLE 20
PUNCHATZ, DON 230
RAGLAND, GREG 93
RAMAGE, ALFRED 124
RHODES, BARBARA 162
RIXFORD, ELLEN 118
SALVATORE, ROSEMARY 207
SCALI, SAM 96
SEIGEL, FRAN 22-33
SMITH, THERESA 176
STEDMAN, EMILY 86
SWAN, SUSAN 121
SWEARINGEN, KAREN MEYER 208
SYMINGTON, GARY 143
TORRISI, GARY 181
WALDMAN, BRYNA 236
WHITESIDES, KIM 68-69
WILCOX, DAVID 38-39
YULE, SUSAN 123

MEDICAL

AMOROSI, THOMAS 191
AMOROSI, TERESA 191
ANDELIN, DOUGLAS 80
BON DURANT, STEVE 160-161
CARBONE, LOUIS 122
CATALANO, SAL 148
COHEN, SHAY 251

DIEFENDORF, CATHY 180
ERICKSON, KERNE 108
GOLDSTEIN, GWEN 180-181
GREGORY, LANE 181
ICON GRAPHICS 160-161
LEVINSON, DAVID 94
MEEHAN, KEITH 161
PUNCHATZ, DON 230
RIXFORD, ELLEN 118
STEDMAN, EMILY 86
TORRISI, GARY 181
WILCOX, DAVID 38-39

NATURE

ABRAMOWITZ FINE ARTS, INC. 222-223
AMOROSI, THOMAS 191
AMOROSI, TERESA 191
ANDELIN, DOUGLAS 80
BOLTON, ANDREA 110
BRALDS, BRALDT 46-47
BROWN, SUE ELLEN 217
CARLSON, FREDERICK 134
CATALANO, SAL 148
CRAFT, KINUKO 22-23
DEETER, CATHERINE 26-27
DEGROAT, DIANE 183
DETRICH, SUSAN 150
DIEFENDORF, CATHY 180
DUDASH, MICHAEL 60
DUFOUR LOVE, JUDITH 153
ERICKSON, KERNE 108
FRALEY, KIM 101
GAY, PATTI 224
GIUSTI, ROBERT 36-37
GOLDSTEIN, GWEN 180-181
GOLDSTROM, ROBERT 49
GRANING, KEN 87
GREGORY, LANE 181
HAMILL, PAUL 209
HESS, MARK 42-43
HOGAN, SHANNON 106
HOKANSON, LARS 28-29
HOWELL, VAN 246
LATTO, SOPHIA 127
LEVY LIBERMAN, JONI 155

LUNDGREN, TIMOTHY 220
LYTLE, JOHN 210
MACEREN, JUDE 113
McENTIRE, LARRY 32-33
McLEAN, WILSON 66-67
MINOR, WENDELL 50-51
MORECRAFT, RON 152
O'KEEFE YOUNG, MARY 199
PEDERSEN, JUDY 56-57
POSEY, PAM 100
PRZEWODEK, CAMILLE 20
PUNCHATZ, DON 230
RHODES, BARBARA 162
SALVATORE, ROSEMARY 207
SCALI, SAM 96
SEIGEL, FRAN 22-33
SIERRA, DOROTHEA 141
SUTTON, JUDITH 146-147
SYSKA, RICHARD 228
TORRES, LEYLA 204
TORRISI, GARY 181
WALDMAN, BRYNA 236
WALTER, NANCY LEE 81
WILCOX, DAVID 38-39

PORTRAIT

ANDELIN, DOUGLAS 80
BARRETT, JACK 133
BLACKWELL, PATRICK 253
BOWLES, BRUCE 198
BROWN, SUE ELLEN 217
BURGIO, TRISH 64-65
CAMARENA, MIGUEL 105
CARLSON, FREDERICK 134
CATALANO, SAL 148
COLE, DICK 169
CRAFT, KINUKO 22-23
DEETER, CATHERINE 26-27
DELUZ, TONY 226
DIEFENDORF, CATHY 180
DOUGHTY, ROBERT 98
DUDASH, MICHAEL 60
EVANS, GLEN 99
FLEMING, DEAN 159
FRALEY, KIM 101

EASY ACCESS INDEX

GALLAGHER, MATTHEW	114
GANTON, CHRISTOPHER	61
GAY, PATTI	224
GENZO, JOHN PAUL	119
GIBBONS, BILL	165
GIUSTI, ROBERT	36-37
GOLDSTEIN, GWEN	180-181
GREGORY, LANE	181
HARRELSON, PAMELA	92
HESS, RICHARD	35
HESS, MARK	42-43
HIROKO	167
HOGAN, SHANNON	106
HOKANSON, LARS	28-29
HOWARD, JOHN	48
HOWELL, VAN	246
JOHNSON, STEPHEN	62-63
JONES, CATHERINE	176
JUHASZ, VICTOR	40-41
KELENY, EARL	30-31
KELLEY, PATRICK	188
LATTO, SOPHIA	127
LEECH, DOROTHY	126
LEVINSON, DAVID	94
LYTLE, JOHN	210
MASCIOVECCHIO, MARIE	254
McLEAN, WILSON	66-67
MILLER, MARCIA	88
MINOR, WENDELL	50-51
MORECRAFT, RON	152
O'KEEFE YOUNG, MARY	199
PEDERSEN, JUDY	56-57
PIETROBONO, JANET	189
POSEY, PAM	100
PRZEWODEK, CAMILLE	20
PUNCHATZ, DON	230
RAGLAND, GREG	93
REINGOLD, ALAN	72
RHODES, BARBARA	162
RIEDY, MARK	239
RIXFORD, ELLEN	118
ROUNDTREE, DEBORAH	21
SCHWARTZ, JUDITH	213
SEIGEL, FRAN	22-33
SIERRA, DOROTHEA	141
SMITH, THERESA	176

SMITH, JEFFREY	242-243
SPELMAN, STEVE	21
STEDMAN, EMILY	86
SWANSON, JAMES	34
SWEARINGEN, KAREN MEYER	208
TAYLOR, C. WINSTON	111
THOMAS, ROD	216
TORRISI, GARY	181
TREATNER, MERYL	170-171
VINCENT, BENJAMIN	240
VON MORISSE, ANDRE	109
WHITESIDES, KIM	68-69
ZWARENSTEIN, ALEX	73

PRODUCT

AMOROSI, THOMAS	191
AMOROSI, TERESA	191
ANDELIN, DOUGLAS	80
BARRETT, JACK	133
BON DURANT, STEVE	160-161
BOWLES, BRUCE	198
CARBONE, LOUIS	122
COHEN, SHAY	251
COLE, DICK	169
DIEFENDORF, CATHY	180
DUGAN, BRIAN	71
ERICKSON, KERNE	108
FERSTER, GARY	132
FLEMING, DEAN	159
GENZO, JOHN PAUL	119
GOLDSTEIN, GWEN	180-181
GRANING, KEN	87
GREGORY, ERRICO	138
GREGORY, LANE	181
HARRELSON, PAMELA	92
HARRISON, HUGH	139
HOGAN, SHANNON	106
HOKANSON, LARS	28-29
ICON GRAPHICS	160-161
JOLY, DAVE	184
JONES, CATHERINE	176
JONES, DANIELLE	234-235
JUST, HAL	73
KELENY, EARL	30-31
LAW, POLLY	202-203

LEVY LIBERMAN, JONI	155
MEEHAN, KEITH	161
MORECRAFT, RON	152
MORRISON, CATHY	244
PIETROBONO, JANET	189
PRENTICE, LYNNE	215
PRZEWODEK, CAMILLE	20
PUNCHATZ, DON	230
RAMAGE, ALFRED	124
REINGOLD, ALAN	72
RHODES, BARBARA	162
RIEDY, MARK	239
ROUNDTREE, DEBORAH	21
RUSSELL, BILL	196
SCHROEDER, MARK	211
SIERRA, DOROTHEA	141
SMITH, THERESA	176
SOKOLOWSKI, TED	247
SPELMAN, STEVE	21
SUTTON, JUDITH	146-147
SYMINGTON, GARY	143
SYSKA, RICHARD	228
TORRISI, GARY	181
ZWARENSTEIN, ALEX	73

ROMANCE

BLACKWELL, PATRICK	253
DIEFENDORF, CATHY	180
DOUGHTY, ROBERT	98
FARACLAS JENNISON, ANDREA	145
GOLDSTEIN, GWEN	180-181
GREGORY, LANE	181
HOGAN, SHANNON	106
LEVY LIBERMAN, JONI	155
LUNDGREN, TIMOTHY	220
McGURL, MICHAEL	151
MINOR, WENDELL	50-51
MORECRAFT, RON	152
PEDERSEN, JUDY	56-57
REINGOLD, ALAN	72
SYSKA, RICHARD	228
TORRISI, GARY	181
TREATNER, MERYL	170-171
WALDMAN, BRYNA	236
WHITESIDES, KIM	68-69

ZWARENSTEIN, ALEX	73

SCIENCE FICTION/ FANTASY

BRALDS, BRALDT	46-47
BROWN, SUE ELLEN	217
CHING, DARREN	186
CRAFT, KINUKO	22-23
DAWSON, JOHN	24-25
DEETER, CATHERINE	26-27
DEGROAT, DIANE	183
DIEFENDORF, CATHY	180
EVANS, GLEN	99
FERSTER, GARY	132
FLEMING, DEAN	159
GAETANO, NICK	237
GIUSTI, ROBERT	36-37
GOLDSTEIN, GWEN	180-181
GREGORY, LANE	181
HOKANSON, LARS	28-29
JONES, CATHERINE	176
JUSKO, JOE	219
KELLEY, PATRICK	188
MACEREN, JUDE	113
McGURL, MICHAEL	151
MELLET-BERRY, FANNY	72
MORECRAFT, RON	152
PUNCHATZ, DON	230
SCALI, SAM	96
SEIGEL, FRAN	22-23
SMITH, THERESA	176
TORRISI, GARY	181
VON MORISSE, ANDRE	109
WALDMAN, BRYNA	236
WALTER, NANCY LEE	81
WINN-LEDERER, ILENE	136

SPORTS

ANDELIN, DOUGLAS	80
BLACKWELL, PATRICK	253
BON DURANT, STEVE	160-161

EASY ACCESS INDEX

BURGIO, TRISH	64-65
CAPPARELLI, TONY	252
CARLSON, FREDERICK	134
CARSON, JIM	194
CLEGG, DAVID	221
CONSOLE, JR., CARMEN	90
DELUZ, TONY	226
DIEFENDORF, CATHY	180
DUDASH, MICHAEL	60
DUGAN, BRIAN	71
ERICKSON, KERNE	108
FERSTER, GARY	132
FOSTER, MATT	248-249
GOLDSTEIN, GWEN	180-181
GREGORY, LANE	181
HARRELSON, PAMELA	92
HESS, MARK	42-43
HOLDER, JIMMY	182
ICON GRAPHICS	160-161
JONES, DANIELLE	234-235
JUHASZ, VICTOR	40-41
KELENY, EARL	30-31
LATTO, SOPHIA	127
LYTLE, JOHN	210
MARTINOT, CLAUDE	74
McDANIEL, JERRY	73
McLEAN, WILSON	66-67
MEEHAN, KEITH	161
MORECRAFT, RON	152
NOISET, MICHELE	76
PUNCHATZ, DON	230
RHODES, BARBARA	162
RIEDY, MARK	239
STANFILL, MIKE	240
SYSKA, RICHARD	228
TORRISI, GARY	181
WHITESIDES, KIM	68-69

STORYBOARDS/ COMPS

AMOROSI, THOMAS	191
AMOROSI, TERESA	191
BYER, LOU	193
DELUZ, TONY	226

DIEFENDORF, CATHY	180
ENOS, RANDALL	70
GREGORY, ERRICO	138
GREGORY, LANE	181
HILL, KENNIE	193
HOGAN, SHANNON	106
LAW, POLLY	202-203
PIETROBONO, JANET	189
TORRISI, GARY	181
VINCENT, BENJAMIN	240
ZWARENSTEIN, ALEX	73

TECHNICAL

AMOROSI, THOMAS	191
AMOROSI, TERESA	191
BYER, LOU	193
COHEN, SHAY	251
DIEFENDORF, CATHY	180
FERSTER, GARY	132
GOLDSTEIN, GWEN	180-181
GREGORY, LANE	181
HILL, KENNIE	193
SCHROEDER, MARK	211
SOKOWLOWSKI, TED	247
STANFILL, MIKE	240
TORRISI, GARY	181
WALTER, NANCY LEE	81

THREE- DIMENSIONAL

ANDELIN, DOUGLAS	80
DIEFENDORF, CATHY	180
GOLDSTEIN, GWEN	180-181
GREGORY, LANE	181
HARRELSON, PAMELA	92
MORECRAFT, RON	152
RIXFORD, ELLEN	118
SWAN, SUSAN	121
THELEN, MARY	225
TORRISI, GARY	181
WILLIAMS, TOBY	154

TRANS- PORTATION

BILLOUT, GUY	197
BLACKWELL, PATRICK	253
BON DURANT, STEVE	160-161
BYER, LOU	193
CARBONE, LOUIS	122
CARSON, JIM	194
CONSOLE, JR., CARMEN	90
DIEFENDORF, CATHY	180
FARACLAS JENNISON, ANDREA	145
FERSTER, GARY	132
GOLDSTROM, ROBERT	49
GRANING, KEN	87
GREGORY, LANE	181
HESS, RICHARD	35
HESS, MARK	42-43
HILL, KENNIE	193
HOWARD, JOHN	43
ICON GRAPHICS	160-161
LAUTENSLAGER, PETER	177
MACHAT, MIKE	104
MARTINOT, CLAUDE	74
MEEHAN, KEITH	161
MORECRAFT, RON	152
POSEY, PAM	100
RIEDY, MARK	239
SMYTH, RICHARD	163
SYMINGTON, GARY	143
SYSKA, RICHARD	228
TORRISI, GARY	181
WILCOX, DAVID	38-39
ZWARENSTEIN, ALEX	73

OTHER

AMOROSI, THOMAS	191
AMOROSI, TERESA	191
BARRERA, POLO	253
BEGO, DOLORES	72
BIANCO, PETER	147
BON DURANT, STEVE	160-161
BYER, LOU	193
CAPPARELLI, TONY	252

CATHCART, MARILYN	154
CHID	125
CHING, DARREN	186
COFFELT, KEN	84-85
COLE, DICK	169
CRAFT, KINUKO	22-23
DAWSON, JOHN	24-25
DOGUE, MAURICE	173
ENOS, RANDALL	70
FOWLER, ERIC	95
FRALEY, KIM	101
GAETANO, NICK	237
GESER, GRETCHEN	122
GIBBONS, BILL	165
GREENSTEIN, SUSAN	129
GREGORY, ERRICO	138
HAMILL, PAUL	209
HARRISON, HUGH	139
HILL, KENNIE	193
HOKANSON, LARS	28-29
HOWELL, VAN	246
ICON GRAPHICS	160-161
JUST, HAL	73
KELENY, EARL	30-31
LAUTENSLAGER, PETER	177
LEVY LIBERMAN, JONI	155
MACEREN, JUDE	145
McDANIEL, JERRY	73
McENTIRE, LARRY	32-33
MEEHAN, KEITH	161
MELLET-BERRY, FANNY	72
MORECRAFT, RON	152
MORRISON, DON	72
PIETROBONO, JANET	189
RAGLAND, GREG	93
RAMAGE, ALFRED	124
RAMSEY, CARL	78-79
SAYAD, MARDUK	166
SEIGEL, FRAN	22-33
SIERRA, DOROTHEA	141
STEDMAN, EMILY	86
SYMINGTON, GARY	143
THORNTON, BLAKE	117
URBANOVIC, JACKIE	77
WINN-LEDERER, ILENE	136

ON JOINING THE GUILD

When you join the Guild, you're making a very definite statement of your conviction that graphic artists deserve the same respect our society affords other professionals.

JOINING THE GUILD affirms the value of artists working *together* to improve standards of pay and working conditions in our industry. Joining is an endorsement of the highest standards of ethical conduct in the marketplace.

JOINING THE GUILD is joining the effort to advance the rights and interests of artist through legislative reform. Examples: our ongoing fight to end the widespread abuse of the copyright law's "work-for-hire" language; our successful battle against unfair taxation of artists.

JOINING THE GUILD may provide you with a vehicle for contract bargaining — with your employer if you are a staff artist, or even with your client if you are one of a group of free-lance artists regularly working for a given client.

JOINING THE GUILD puts you in contact with other artists who share your concerns. It's a way to share ideas, information, and business skills with your colleagues.

JOINING THE GUILD has immediate practical benefits.

. . .

☆ Members receive the latest edition of the *Graphic Artists Guild Handbook, Pricing & Ethical Guidelines*. This best-seller contains a wealth of information about pricing and trade practices in every corner of the graphic arts. Many consider it an industry "Bible."

☆ Group Health Insurance as well as disability and retirement plans are available to members at favorable rates.

☆ Members receive a subscription to national and local chapter newsletters.

☆ Your local chapter may provide direct marketing assistance through job referral services, trade shows and other activities.

☆ Members receive substantial discounts on supplies from many dealers, and on pagerates in many illustration and design directories.

☆ Chapters also run "hotlines" to give members access to advice and referrals to Guild-approved lawyers and accountants should you need them.

☆ Chapters produce educational programs and social events for members.

. . .

The Graphic Artists Guild is the only organization of its kind in the United States. If you want to work together with other artists to effect positive change in the status of artists in the marketplace and in society, YOU BELONG IN THE GUILD!

PLEASE PHOTOCOPY THIS PAGE, FILL OUT ALL PORTIONS OF THIS FORM AND MAIL IT WITH YOUR DUES PAYMENT AND INITIATION FEE TO:

MEMBERSHIP STATUS

Guild Membership comprises two categories: Member and Associate Member. Only working graphic artists are eligible to become full Members. Interested People in related fields who support the goals and purposes of the Guild are welcome to join as Associate Members, as are graphic arts students and retired artists. Associate Members may participate in all Guild activities and programs, but not hold office or vote.

The Graphic Artists Guild is a national organization with local chapters. Membership applications are processed at the national office; you'll be enrolled either in a local chapter serving your area or in the "At-Large" chapter if there is no local chapter near you.

○ I earn more than half of my income from my own graphic work, and am therefore eligible to join the Guild as a Member.

○ I wish to join the Guild as an Associate Member.

**GRAPHIC ARTISTS GUILD
11 WEST 20TH STREET, 8TH FLOOR
NEW YORK, NY 10011-3704**

NAME _____

ADDRESS _____

CITY _____ STATE _____ ZIP _____

BUSINESS PHONE _____ HOME PHONE _____

DISCIPLINE(S)

Please mark "1" for the area in which you do most of your work, and "2" and "3" for additional specialties.

● GRAPHIC DESIGN

● ILLUSTRATION

● PRE-PRODUCTION ART

● SURFACE DESIGN

● CARTOONING

● PHOTOGRAPHY

● COMPUTER ARTS

● PRODUCTION/MECHANICALS

● ART DIRECTION

● ARTISTS' REPRESENTATIVE

● TEACHING PROFESSIONAL

● VIDEO/BROADCAST DESIGN

● OTHER _____

_____

_____

MEMBERSHIP STATEMENT

Please read and sign the following:

I derive more income from my own work as a graphic artist than I do from the owner or manager of any business which profits from the buying and/or selling of graphic artwork.*

I, the undersigned, agree to abide by the Constitution of the Graphic Artists Guild and do hereby authorize the Guild to act as my representative with regard to negotiation of agreements approved by the Guild membership to improve pricing and ethical standards of the graphic arts profession.**

I further understand that my membership in the Graphic Artists Guild is continuous and that I will be billed for membership dues annually on the anniversary of my original application. If I wish to resign from the Graphic Artists Guild, I understand that I must resign in writing, and that I will be responsible for the payment of any dues owned prior to the date of my resignation.

*This statement does not apply to associate members.

**Your membership package will contain a copy of the constitution. To obtain one prior to joining, send $1 with your request to the national office. The document is also on file at national and chapter offices for inspection.

SIGNATURE _____ DATE _____

DUES AND INITIATION FEE

To offset the administrative expense of processing new memberships, the Guild collects a $25. one-time fee with membership application. ■ Guild dues depend upon membership category and income level. Income level refers to your total adjusted gross income from your federal tax return.

Member Dues (Please Check Category):

☐ Income under $12,000/yr ... $100 per year

☐ Income $12,000-30,000/yr .. $135 per year

☐ Income over $30,000/yr ...... $175 per year

Associate Member Dues:

☐ Students .... $55 per year

☐ Others .... $95 per year

Method of Payment

☐ Check ☐ Money Order

Dues* _____

Initiation Fee   **$25**

Total enclosed _____

*You may remit one-half of your dues with this application (plus the initiation fee), we will bill you for the second half, which must be paid within 120 days.

Returned checks are subject to $10 service charge.

On occasion, the Guild allows the use of its mailing list by companies selling products of interest to our members. Please check this box if you do not wish to have your name made available in this manner. ☐

EMPLOYMENT STATUS

If you are on staff and do freelance work as well, please mark "1" for staff and "2" for freelance.

○ STAFF ○ RETIRED GRAPHIC ARTIST

○ FREELANCE (includes business owners, partners, and corporation principals)

○ STUDENT

School _____

Year of graduation _____

(Students must include a photocopy of current college I.D.)

For office use only: PEGS_____ MEMBERSHIP CARD_____ AZW_____

THE GUILD

This year marks the 25th anniversary of the Graphic Artists Guild. A milestone in our history, the Guild's Silver Anniversary is cause for celebration—not only for what we've accomplished over the years, but also for new undertakings which signify the Guild's growth and importance in the industry.

Perhaps most important among the Guild's accomplishments is the publication of the *Graphic Artists Guild Handbook, Pricing & Ethical Guidelines*. The current 7th edition, released in May, 1991, is being readied for a third printing early in 1992. With over 43,000 copies of this edition already in print, the *P.E.G.s* (which contains an excellent section on illustration), is clearly accepted as the industry's primary reference for pricing guidelines and professional standards and practices.

Noted illustrator Marshall Arisman (Guild member since 1982), recently said that if the *Guild Handbook, Pricing & Ethical Guidelines* were the only thing the Guild ever accomplished, that alone would justify our existence. But we've accomplished a great deal more.

- Thanks to our persistence, the return of the original artwork is now an accepted industry practice, and "Fair Practices" is law in New York, California, Oregon and other states.

- We've made steady progress in resisting work for hire by testifying time and time again in support of legislation which we helped draft.

- We also helped convince the Supreme Court to favorably decide (in CCNV v. Reid) to virtually eliminate work for hire without a written agreement.

- Our legislative victory on Uniform Tax Capitalization will save artists thousands of tax dollars for years to come.

From its inception, the Guild has been dedicated to uniting all professional artists and designers within the communications industry; advancing their economic and social interests; establishing and maintaining educational, recreational, social and charitable enterprises that help them advance professionally and aid their general welfare; and promoting and maintaining high professional standards of ethics and practices.

To these ends, the Guild's first national conference is scheduled for June 11–14, 1992 in Washington, D.C. Appropriately, "Eye to Eye" (as we're calling it) will look back on the Guild's first 25 years as artists' advocate and focus on its role for the next 25 years. The conference's mission statement elaborates on its theme:

As soon as individuals come eye to eye, the search for common ground begins. The Graphic Artists Guild's first national conference will bring graphic artists together to focus on the business, economic and creative issues surrounding their work. Those who attend will be inspired by contact with leaders in their field and become galvanized in their efforts to secure a better work climate for artists and clients. By standing shoulder to shoulder and seeing eye to eye, artists will develop new tools for coping with a rapidly changing global economy.

A new, but no less important, undertaking appears on the overleaf. For the first time, the Guild is actively promoting the talents of its illustrator members to those who use their services by sponsoring this advertisement which seeks to heighten the awareness of illustration as an important communications tool. We are proud to feature this in the *Graphic Artists Guild Directory of Illustration #8*.

Isolation is the most difficult part of being an illustrator. That's why the Guild was structured to promote opportunities for networking, sharing information and overcoming the disadvantages of isolation in a constantly shrinking world. Always a bottom-up organization, Guild members initiate and execute all Guild activities and projects.

Guild members enjoy national and chapter newsletters, insurance programs and member discounts (like the discount on the page rate in this *Directory of Illustration*). Local chapters offer the services, programs and events that meet the needs of artists who, for the most part, work alone. These include the opportunity to network, take business courses, resolve disputes with clients or discuss relevant career issues with peers. And on the national level, the Guild monitors legislative and industry activity while working hard to unite its chapters and members for the common good.

The Guild's Silver Anniversary is certainly cause for celebration. But to us, it's a stepping stone to a golden future for the organization, its members and the industry.

Paul Basista
National Executive Director

A TIME WHOSE ADVERTISING AGENCY HAS COME.

But until today, our phones hadn't. Nor did we have an address.

Still they found us.

At first by the score, then into the hundreds. Letters and resumes arrived at our homes in bundles, phone messages grew to staggering stacks.

What started as a drizzle became a full-fledged flood.

Why all the interest in us? An ad agency that had yet to open, let alone land a big account?

Obviously many advertising people are in need of work. And ours isn't the only door being beaten upon.

But we've also been besieged by people who are far from needy. Many have told us that they're happy in their present jobs but would take salary cuts for the chance to work with us.

More than a few free-lancers have offered to help out free. To get in on the ground floor.

Of course quite a few of the calls and letters have been coming from potential clients.

Some are advertisers who have seen that too much energy has been going into the business of advertising rather than the creation of it.

Others are fed up with having their accounts shunted around from place to place, like chattel.

Some have simply come to realize that a talented and dedicated owner-management might serve them better than any far-flung faceless empire with a vast array of disjointed services.

Prospects. Job seekers. Vendors. They've all witnessed, and suffered from, the tumult that has beset advertising for the past few years. And they've been waiting, hoping for something new, something better.

To all the advertisers, applicants, brokers, media, employment agents,

suppliers and friends with whom we've had contact since we announced our intent to embark on this enterprise: we thank you.

We thank you for your interest, your enthusiasm, and your excitement.

But most of all, we want to thank you for your hope.

Even though this may not seem like the best of times to launch a new business, we have high hopes for success.

We also have a plan. It's as simple as one, two, three.

1. Do great work.
2. Clients come and grow.
3. Fortune follows.

That's our story and we're sticking to it.

If you'd like to know more, give us a call. And if you have trouble getting through at first, please be patient.

We've been swamped.

McCABE & COMPANY

101 EAST 52ND STREET, NEW YORK, NY 10022 TELEPHONE: (212) 308-3434 FAX (212) 308-3520.

This could be the single biggest ad of Ed McCabe's career.

He went with an illustration.

Naturally, Ed had all the right words. What he needed was the right visual, one that would communicate succinctly and graphically, one that would be imaginative and powerful yet one he could control. He could have gone with a photograph. But he didn't. He went with an illustration. And who's going to argue with Ed McCabe, especially when he's right.

ILLUSTRATION.
The Original Visual.

This ad is sponsored by the Graphic Artists Guild. Special thanks to: Ed McCabe, McCabe & Company; Arnie Arlow, Creative/Art Director; David Warren, Copywriter; Cathie Bleck, Illustrator (represented by Jacqueline Dedell, Inc.).

DEBORAH *Roundtree*

SPEL·MAN

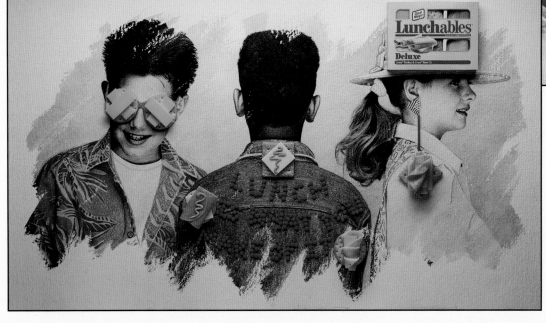

108 East 35 St.
New York 10016
Phone: (212) 889-3337
Fax: (212) 889-3341

GERALD & CULLEN RAPP, INC.

CREATIVE OPTION TRADERS

Wines of Spain

Wines of Spain

Crabtree & Evelyn

McLelland & Stewart

Fran Seigel 515 Madison Ave. New York, NY 10022 (212) 486-9644

Harrowsmith Magazine

Fran Seigel   515 Madison Ave. New York, NY 10022   (212) 486-9644

HBJ (Alice Walker Picture Book)

Macmillan Publishing

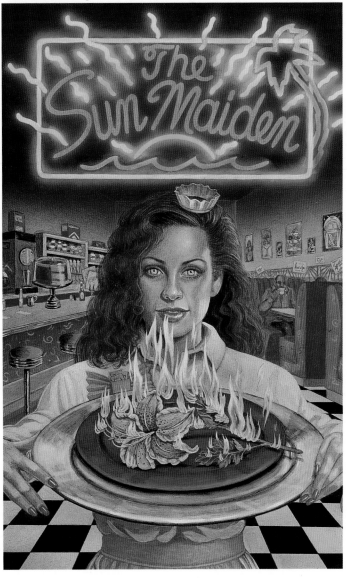

Fran Seigel   515 Madison Ave. New York, NY 10022   (212) 486-9644

Lars Hokanson

William Collins & Sons

JWT/Kalle Infotec

JWT/Kalle Infotec

Fran Seigel   515 Madison Ave. New York, NY 10022   (212) 486-9644

29

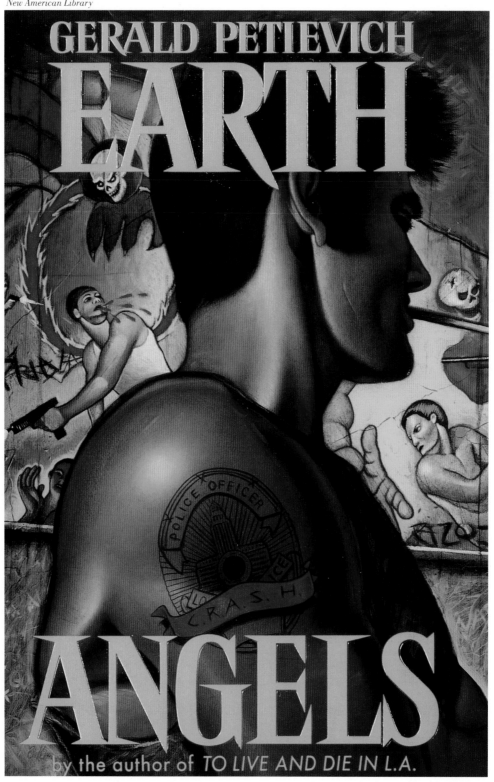

Northwestern Mutual Life Insurance

Northwestern Mutual Life Insurance

Fran Seigel   515 Madison Ave.   New York, NY 10022   (212) 486-9644

Fran Seigel 515 Madison Ave. New York, NY 10022 (212) 486-9644

Vermont Magazine

33

Ford (advertorial)

Kelly Communications

Changing Times

Outside Magazine

Fran Seigel   515 Madison Ave. New York, NY 10022   (212) 486-9644

James Swanson (708) 383-0141

R I C H A R D   H E S S

310 LITCHFIELD ROAD
NORFOLK, CONNECTICUT 06058
(203) 542-5529 FAX (203) 542-5520

In Memory of
RICHARD HESS
1934-1991

Represented by:
MILTON NEWBORN ASSOCIATES
135 EAST 54TH STREET
NEW YORK, NEW YORK 10022
(212) 421-0050 FAX (212) 421-0444

R O B E R T   G I U S T I

340 LONG MOUNTAIN ROAD
NEW MILFORD, CONNECTICUT 06776
TEL. & FAX (203) 354-6539

Represented by:
MILTON NEWBORN ASSOCIATES
135 EAST 54TH STREET
NEW YORK, NEW YORK 10022
(212) 421-0050 FAX (212) 421-0444

DOM KOLSCH

GENERAL ELECTRIC

BRITISH AIRWAYS

R O B E R T   G I U S T I

340 LONG MOUNTAIN ROAD
NEW MILFORD, CONNECTICUT 06776
TEL. & FAX (203) 354-6539

Represented by:
MILTON NEWBORN ASSOCIATES
135 EAST 54TH STREET
NEW YORK, NEW YORK 10022
(212) 421-0050 FAX (212) 421-0444

MATSON LINES

OMNI THEATER

AIR CANADA

TACTYLON

D A V I D W I L C O X

5955 SAWMILL ROAD
DOYLESTOWN, PENNSYLVANIA 18901
TEL. & FAX (215) 297-0849

Represented by:
MILTON NEWBORN ASSOCIATES
135 EAST 54TH STREET
NEW YORK, NEW YORK 10022
(212) 421-0050 FAX (212) 421-0444

HARMAN/KARDON

NEWSWEEK

G.T.E.

PENGUIN/NAL

D A V I D W I L C O X

5955 SAWMILL ROAD
DOYLESTOWN, PENNSYLVANIA 18901
TEL. & FAX (215) 297-0849

Represented by:
MILTON NEWBORN ASSOCIATES
135 EAST 54TH STREET
NEW YORK, NEW YORK 10022
(212) 421-0050 FAX (212) 421-0444

CHASE BANK

AMERICAN DENTAL ASS'N

PLAYBOY

BROWN & ROOT

576 WESTMINSTER AVE.
ELIZABETH, NEW JERSEY 07208
(908) 351-4227 FAX (908) 355-0179

Represented by:
MILTON NEWBORN ASSOCIATES
135 EAST 54TH STREET
NEW YORK, NEW YORK 10022
(212) 421-0050 FAX (212) 421-0444

576 WESTMINSTER AVE.
ELIZABETH, NEW JERSEY 07208
(908) 351-4227 FAX (908) 355-0179

Represented by:
MILTON NEWBORN ASSOCIATES
135 EAST 54TH STREET
NEW YORK, NEW YORK 10022
(212) 421-0050 FAX (212) 421-0444

OXFORD UNIVERSITY PRESS

INVESTMENT VISION

RENT STABILIZATION ASS'N.

MERRILL LYNCH

MARK HESS

88 QUICKS LANE
KATONAH, NEW YORK 10536
TEL. & FAX (914) 232-5870

Represented by:
MILTON NEWBORN ASSOCIATES
135 EAST 54TH STREET
NEW YORK, NEW YORK 10022
(212) 421-0050 FAX (212) 421-0444

ANHEUSER-BUSCH, INC.

HARROWSMITH

BRIGHAM YOUNG UNIVERSITY

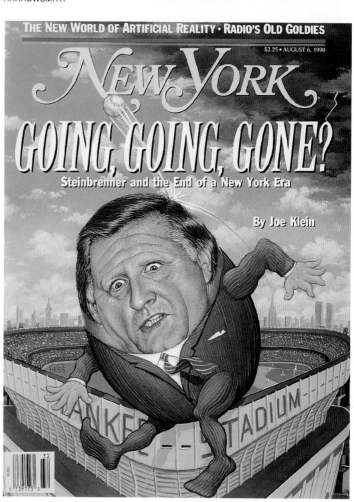

NEW YORK MAGAZINE

M A R K   H E S S

88 QUICKS LANE
KATONAH, NEW YORK 10536
TEL. & FAX (914) 232-5870

Represented by:
MILTON NEWBORN ASSOCIATES
135 EAST 54TH STREET
NEW YORK, NEW YORK 10022
(212) 421-0050 FAX (212) 421-0444

WARNER BOOKS

OCE COPIERS

ATHENEUM BOOKS

NOTRE DAME MAGAZINE

What would you like to buy to eat? If this were your neighborhood grocery store, what foods would you find?

SUPPLEMENT TO SCHOLASTIC LET'S FIND OUT · NOV./DEC. 1990
ILLUSTRATED BY SIMMS TABACK

SCHOLASTIC

SCHOLASTIC

15 WEST 20TH STREET
NEW YORK, NEW YORK 10011
(212) 627-5220 FAX (212) 206-0052

Represented by:
MILTON NEWBORN ASSOCIATES
135 EAST 54TH STREET
NEW YORK, NEW YORK 10022
(212) 421-0050 FAX (212) 421-0444

PEPSI COLA

CARDTRICKS

BRALDT BRALDS

119 WYKEHAM ROAD
WASHINGTON, CONNECTICUT 06793
(203) 868-7577   FAX (203) 868-7060

Represented by:
MILTON NEWBORN ASSOCIATES
135 EAST 54TH STREET
NEW YORK, NEW YORK 10022
(212) 421-0050   FAX (212) 421-0444

NATIONAL SCIENCE FOUNDATION

DAW-BOOKS

PLAYBOY

R.R. DONELLEY & SONS

119 WYKEHAM ROAD
WASHINGTON, CONNECTICUT 06793
(203) 868-7577   FAX (203) 868-7060

Represented by:
MILTON NEWBORN ASSOCIATES
135 EAST 54TH STREET
NEW YORK, NEW YORK 10022
(212) 421-0050 FAX (212) 421-0444

ALFA ROMEO

J O H N H . H O W A R D

336 EAST 54TH STREET
NEW YORK, NEW YORK 10022
(212) 832-7980

Represented by:
JOAN SIGMAN
135 EAST 54TH STREET
NEW YORK, NEW YORK 10022
(212) 421-0050 FAX (212) 421-0444

CAPITAL/BLUENOTE RECORDS

7 DAYS

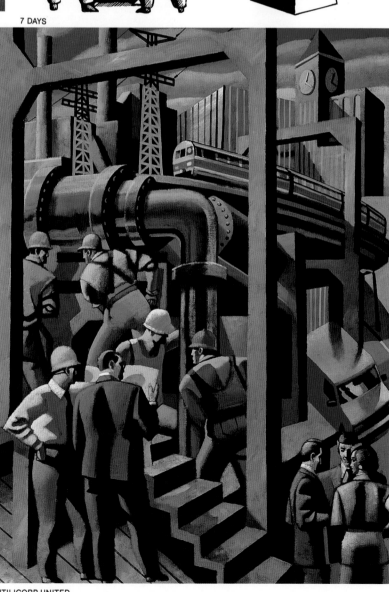

PAN BOOKS LTD.

UTILICORP UNITED

ROBERT GOLDSTROM

471 FIFTH STREET
BROOKLYN, NEW YORK 11215
(718) 768-7367

Represented by:
JOAN SIGMAN
135 EAST 54TH STREET
NEW YORK, NEW YORK 10022
(212) 421-0050 FAX (212) 421-0444

AVON BOOKS

HARROWSMITH

EMERGENCY MEDICINE MAGAZINE

COYOTE TEQUILA

YANKEE MAGAZINE

HARPERCOLLINS

WENDELL MINOR · 15 OLD NORTH ROAD · P.O.B. 1135 · WASHINGTON, CT · 06793 · 203 868-9101 · FAX 868-9512

WENDELL MINOR · 15 OLD NORTH ROAD · P.O.B. 1135 · WASHINGTON, CT · 06793 · 203 868-9101 · FAX 868-9512

Reynold Ruffins
15 West 20th Street
New York, NY 10011

(212) 627-5220

BASEMAN

BASEMAN

IN THE EAST
STUDIO 718.499.9358

IN THE WEST
JAN COLLIER 415.552.4252

JUDY PEDERSEN

305 SECOND AVE. #710
NEW YORK, NY 10003
212·777·8077

JUDY PEDERSEN

305 SECOND AVE. #710
NEW YORK, NY 10003
212·777·8077

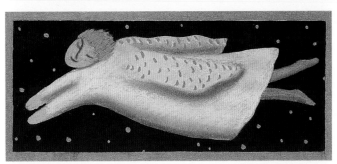

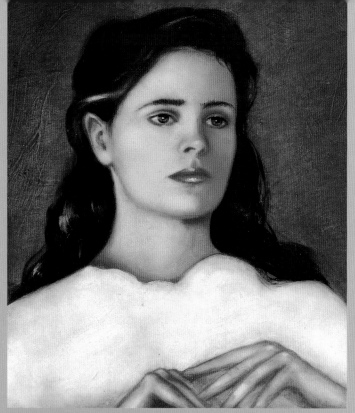

DEBORAH
H·E·A·L·Y

72 WATCHUNG AVENUE
UPPER MONTCLAIR, NJ 07043

201 746 2549

DEBORAH
H·E·A·L·Y

72 WATCHUNG AVENUE
UPPER MONTCLAIR, NJ 07043
201 746 2549

C · MICHAEL · DUDASH

BILL ERLACHER ARTISTS ASSOCIATES   211 E 51 STREET NEW YORK NY 10022   212 · 755 · 1365/6

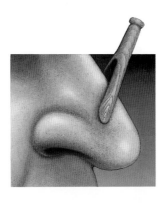

CHRISTOPHER

GANTON

13 Marion Road

Verona, New Jersey 07044

201.857.1381

STEPHEN JOHNSON

81 Remsen Street ▼ Apt.1 ▼ Brooklyn ▼ New York ▼ 11201 ▼ 718/237-2352

STEPHEN JOHNSON

81 Remsen Street ▾ Apt.1 ▾ Brooklyn ▾ New York ▾ 11201 ▾ 718/237-2352

BURGIO

WHEN THE PROBLEM IS MOTHERS AND DAUGHTERS, NEW STUDIES ARE FINDING THAT CUTTING THE CORD ISN'T THE SOLUTION. GETTING CLOSER IS

BUSINESS Marketing
A CRAIN COMMUNICATIONS INC PUBLICATION • JULY 1990 • $3.50

SALES MANGEMENT
Hiring Tests: Dream or Nightmare?

Advertising: How to Grab a Winning Position
Secrets of Sales Motivation
Sales Automation: Doing the Hard Work Right

OUR LIST OF THE TOP 100 BUSINESS-TO-BUSINESS ADVERTISERS

Illustrations by Trish Burgio

WHEN DAISY POM... senior at Northw... in high school, everything ... mother irritated her. She ha... her mother walked and cou... the way she asked a questio... describes their relationship ... rocky." But going away to c... Pommer appreciate her mot... ized how incredibly smart s... good she is with people," sh...

College offered Tracy Bla... who graduated from Yale la... respite. She and her mother... not on the best of terms wh... for school. "There was a lot... in my life that I kept from h... leading a lifestyle she could... stand," says Blackmer, who... Tracy's mother, Pat, admits,... part there was some sense ... sight, out of mind. I didn't h... worry about her as much."... the first couple of years wer... in the end the space that col... vided both women was bene... today they both feel "very g... their relationship.

Maryrose Basi, a senior a... Fisher College, in Rochester... York, had always enjoyed a ... tionship with her mother. W... was growing up, they had di... everything together, from li... sex. Then, when she left for...

...cisely what leads to argument. We tend to get angriest with those whose opinions we value most, and the wish for agreement between mothers and... her daughter's reply.

Mothers, meanwhile, may also need time to adjust to the new dynamics of the rela- tionship. "Everyone thinks that people with absorbing careers don't feel the empty-nest syndrome, but I disagree," says Pommer's mother, Linda Nochlin, a professor of art history. "Things with Daisy are kind of intense when we're together, and I miss her terribly when she leaves. For me, it's wrenching."

Sometimes conflict occurs when mothers and daughters aren't ready to make the transi- tion at the same time. Aryani Ong, a senior at the University of California, Berkeley and an *In View* stringer, found that growing up meant distancing her- self—literally. When she was younger, she says, her mother, a homemaker, was "very protective and wanted to be a part of all aspects of my life." Koei Hie Ong urged her daughter to attend a col- lege 20 minutes away from the family's home in Houston. "But I knew I had to get out of Texas or I wouldn't develop," Aryani says. Her mother predicted she would be ready to transfer to a home- town school by the spring semester. "I was very insecure and dependent as a freshman," Aryani admits. "But I think I stuck it out because I realized my mother didn't think I could do it."

The most important shift that takes

...We tend to get angriest with those whose opinions we value most, and the wish for agreement between mothers and... her own decisions. She needed her independence and autonomy.

"Okay," Scarf said cautiously. "What do you plan to do?"
"Come home," was

"**A**nyone who says there isn't tension ... a daughter goes away to college isn't being totally truthful."

BTURRIGSIHO

8205 Santa Monica Blvd., Ste. #1 - 244, Los Angeles, CA 90046
2 1 3 - 6 5 7 - 1 4 6 9

WILSON McLEAN

902 BROADWAY, SUITE 1603 NEW YORK, N.Y. 10010   (212) 473-5554

WILSON McLEAN
902 BROADWAY, SUITE 1603 NEW YORK, N.Y. 10010 (212) 473-5554

WHITESIDES

Represented by France Aline, Inc. 213 933 2500

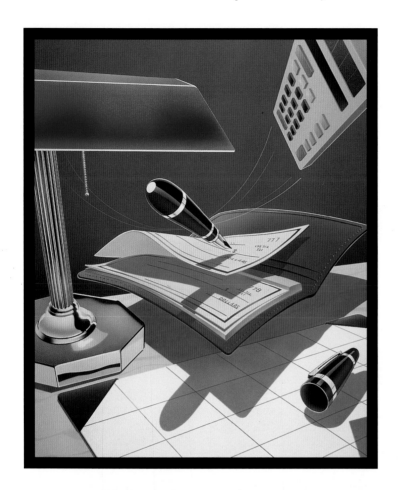

WHITESIDES

STUDIO: 801-649-0490 / FAX: 801-649-9656

Renard Represents
Tel: (212) 490-2450
Fax: (212) 697-6828

Randall Enos

11 COURT OF OAKS
WESTPORT, CT 06880

PHONE & FAX (203) 227-7684

Clients include: Time, Newsweek, Atlantic, New York Times, Washington Post, Boston Globe, McGraw-Hill, Simon and Schuster, Whittle Communications, Pentagram Design, Tennis Magazine, Boy's Life, U.S. News and World Report, Travel Holiday, Hill Holliday Advertising, Post Graduate Medicine, CBS Records, The Nation, The Progressive, Think, Exxon, Mobil, Texaco, Money, Wall St. Journal, Runner's World, Global Finance, Amiga World, Byte, P.C. Week, AT&T, Deutsch Design, Unixworld, Digital Equipment Corp.

THE NEW REPUBLIC

ALAN REINGOLD

DON MORRISON

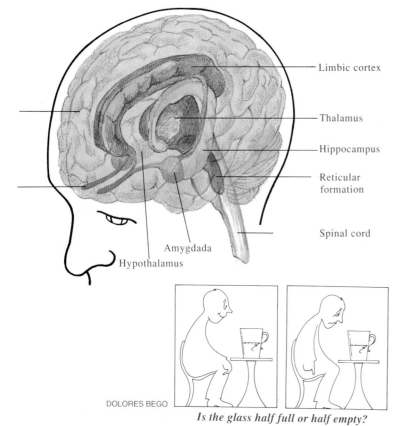

Limbic cortex

Thalamus

Hippocampus

Reticular
formation

Spinal cord

Amygdada

Hypothalamus

DOLORES BEGO

Is the glass half full or half empty?

FANNY MELLET BERRY

Anita Grien
155 East 38th Street
New York, NY 10016

(212) 697-6170
Fax: (212) 697-6177

Representing:

ALAN REINGOLD
DON MORRISON
DOLORES BEGO
FANNY MELLET BERRY

HAL JUST

JERRY MCDANIEL ILLUSTRATION & COMPUTER ART

ALEX ZWARENSTEIN

JULIE JOHNSON

Claude Martinot

CLAUDE MARTINOT DESIGN
H: 145 SECOND AVENUE
NEW YORK, NY 10003
(212) 473-3137

Studio: 1133 Broadway, Suite #1019
New York, NY 10010
(212) 645-0097
Fax (212) 691-3657

Member of the Graphic Artists Guild.

A partial list of my clients: Chase Manhattan Bank, Brooklyn Botanic Garden, The Bronx Zoo, The Federal Reserve Bank of New York, Hallmark Cards, Macmillan Publishing Co., New York Magazine, Silver Burdett & Ginn, Scholastic, Yale University.

My work can also be seen in American Showcase 6, 7, 8, 9, 11, The GAG Directory of Illustration 6, 7, 8, The Creative Illustration Book 1992, RSVP 15, 16, 17.

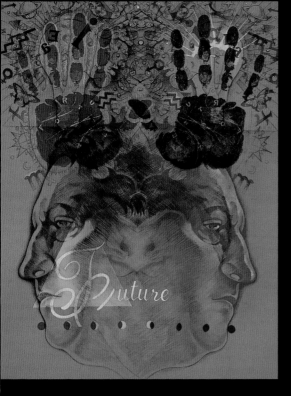

Future

I llustration

PG&E

BANK OF AMERICA

FIREMAN'S FUND

WELLS FARGO BANK

EUREKA BANK

PACIFIC BELL

CHEVRON

CLOROX

INTEL

HILLS BROTHERS

ACUSON

HEWLETT PACKARD

SARN   415-928-1602

M I C H E L E
NOISET
617-542-2731
FAX-422-0298

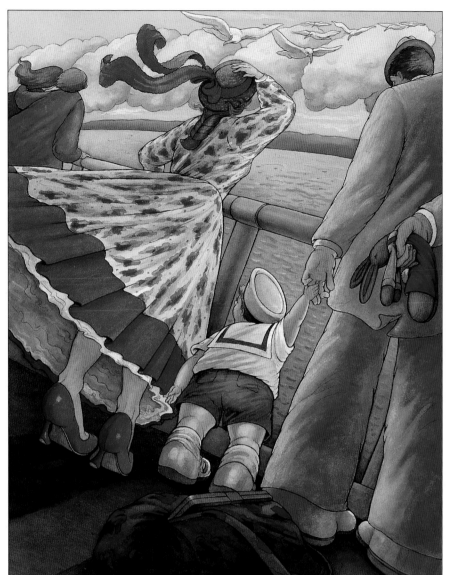

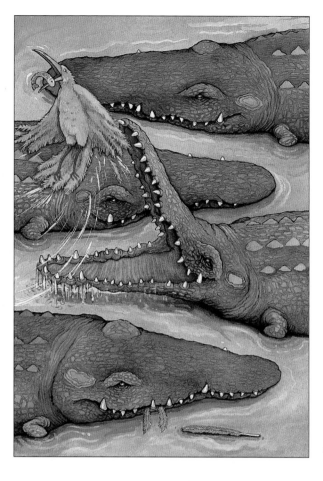

MIDWEST REPRESENTATION
KORALIK ASSOCIATES
312-944-5680
FAX-421-5948

Richfield Bank

Maryland National Bank

THIS IS MARY WOODS, HOW MAY I HELP YOU ??

LOANS

Indiana University Press

Carlson Marketing Group

My Mascot

Corporate Report Minnesota

CARL RAMSEY

213 · 934 · 3150 : STUDIO
213 · 934 · 2248 : FAX

Douglas Andelin

415.550.7625

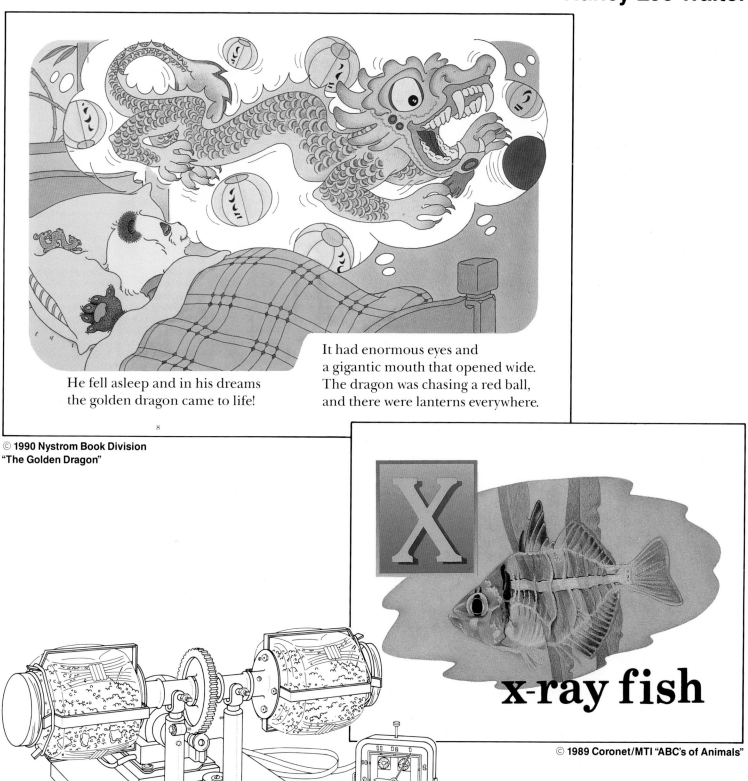

It had enormous eyes and
a gigantic mouth that opened wide.
The dragon was chasing a red ball,
and there were lanterns everywhere.

He fell asleep and in his dreams
the golden dragon came to life!

8

© 1990 Nystrom Book Division
"The Golden Dragon"

x-ray fish

© 1989 Coronet/MTI "ABC's of Animals"

© 1990 Motorola Museum of Electronics

Nancy Lee Walter

391 POPLAR AVENUE
ELMHURST, ILLINOIS 60126-4011

(708) 833-3898
FAX (708) 833-6685

Art for film, video and print: cartoon-style children's and editorial subjects, science, animals. Watercolor, gouache, ink, graphite, colored pencil, and combinations. Samples are available upon request.

Accounts: Lincoln Park Zoo • Motorola Museum of Electronics • General Exhibits & Displays • Coronet/MTI Film and Video • Nystrom • World Book • Childcraft • Encyclopedia Britannica/Comptons • Scott, Foresman

and Company • The Quarasan Group, Inc. • Publicom, Inc. • David C. Cook Publishing Co. • Mlodock Hansen • Vogele Stoic Associates, Inc. • Garfield Linn & Company • Wells, Rich, Green, Inc.

MARK KINGSLEY BROWN
CARTOON ILLUSTRATION

1400 NORTH HIGHWAY 101
LEUCADIA, CALIFORNIA, U.S.A. 92024-1134
TELEPHONE (619) 753-5196
FACSIMILE (619) 753-1953

ANIMALS,

PEOPLE,

THINGS.

DDB / Needham

More Direct

Sefton Associates

Women's Day

BHN

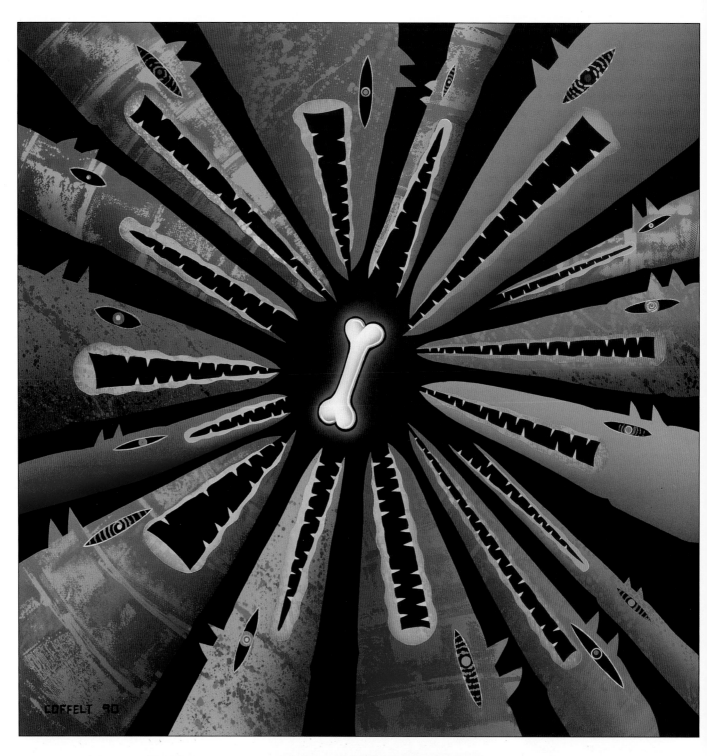

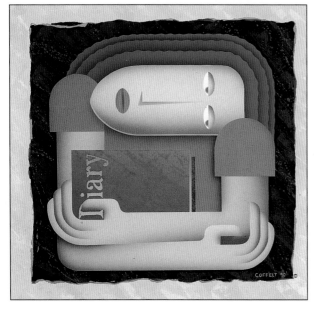

CONTINUUM

Volume 8 Number 1   A Publication of the Continuum Company   Spring, 1990

Legislation
COST CONTROL
GLOBALIZATION
Service
new products
Competition
1992

COFFELT

Ken Coffelt

illustrator

Los Angeles

California

818 | 884-4274

Fax: 818 | 884-3937

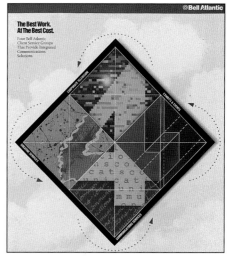

Communicate. Cooperate. Connect. That's what companies are doing with computers in today's complex business environment. Because when your computers work together in a network, you've got a high-performance tool for boosting productivity.

But building a network you can rely on is getting more difficult every day. That's why Compaq and Novell have formed a partnership that's ready to help do the job right.

Compaq is at the forefront of PC connectivity. In fact, we're the leader in high-performance PC network servers. But we're not here on our own. We work closely every step of the way with leading software companies to make sure you get optimum performance and reliability from your network.

Novell, the leader in network operating systems, works closely with Compaq, to deliver reliable, full-function networking capabilities.

Made for each other.

When you run with Novell NetWare on a COMPAQ platform, you're using products that were made for each other. Literally.

That's because Compaq gets involved with Novell's new product development early on—and vice versa. This way, each

COMPAQ

Teamwork. It gets things done faster. It gets things done better. Which is why companies today are demanding teamwork from their computers as well as from their people. You start by connecting your computers together. You end up with a high-performance PC team your people can use to boost productivity.

The only catch is that it's becoming more difficult to configure that team for optimum performance. But there's a company that's ready to make it easier for you now—Compaq.

As a leader in high-performance PC products for the UNIX world, Compaq has been an expert connectivity company for years. But we didn't get here all alone. We teamed up with leading software companies a long time ago. To bring you the highest performance multiuser systems possible.

In fact, our most valuable teammate in the UNIX market is SCO—the leader in multiuser operating systems.

Compaq-SCO teamwork.

Consider what each brings to this team. Compaq provides the highest performance PC platforms from high-end desktops to PC systems; SCO provides one of the highest performance multiuser operating systems. Our goal is to make these strengths stronger, by creating the most powerful, flexible and reliable products.

COMPAQ

Make the right connections. They say that's how to get ahead in business. And today they mean computers, too. Because when you make the right connections between your computers, you've made a high performance network that can help your business be its best.

The only problem is knowing which connections are the right ones to make. But there's a company that's working to help you deal with that problem today—Compaq.

Compaq has set the PC connectivity standard for years as the leader in PC network servers. But we didn't get here on our own. We too made the right connections by working closely with leading network software companies, to bring you the highest performance networking solutions possible.

In fact, one of our tightest connections in the network world is Microsoft—the operating system pioneer.

The Compaq-Microsoft connection.

Compaq and Microsoft work together to plan product development early on, each side contributing its own special networking expertise. This enables both companies to create products that complement each other.

For starters, we worked together on developing Microsoft LAN Manager Version 2.0 to take full advantage of the high-performance capabilities of COMPAQ 486- and 386-based PCs.

COMPAQ

Emily Stedman
(212) 941-0137
474 Greenwich Street, New York, NY 10013

Illustration·Commissions

Fax (212) 941-0140

KEN GRANING
1975 CRAGIN DRIVE/ BLOOMFIELD HILLS, MICHIGAN 48302
■ (313) 851-3665/ FAX: 851-1828

Marcia Miller
124 WEST 79TH STREET
NEW YORK, NEW YORK 10024

(212) 874-6441

Clients include: Macmillan, Ballantine
Books, Dutton Children's Books, Good
Housekeeping Magazine, Family Circle
Magazine, Victoria Magazine, private
and corporate commissioned portraits.

Member of the Graphic Artists Guild

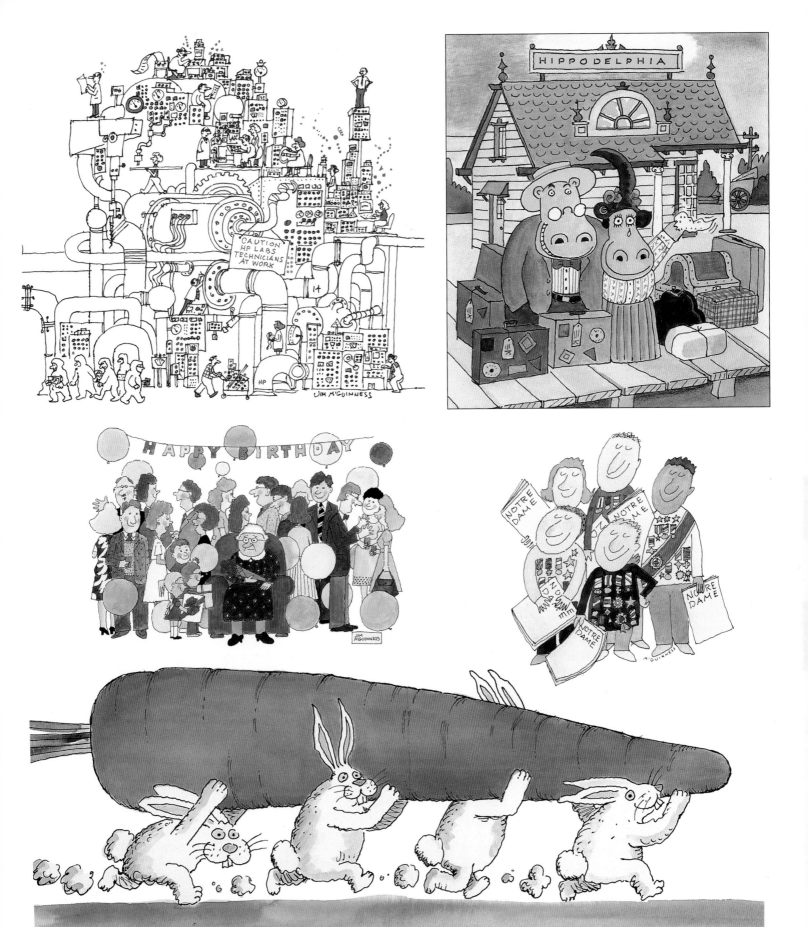

Jim M'Guinness

1122 Golden Way
Los Altos, CA 94024

(415) 967-3811
Fax (415) 968-0967

Illustrations by Jim M'Guinness have captivated audiences from the boardroom to the classroom for many years. He grabs the essence of his client's message whether for an annual report, a magazine ad, a U.S. Postal card or zany characters for a children's book.

From his Silicon Valley studio in the San Francisco Bay Area, he offers a solid array of visual delights.

Partial client list: Cosmopolitan, Hewlett-Packard, IBM, Klutz Press, Random House, Stanford University, J. Walter Thompson, U.S. Postal Service, University of Notre Dame, Woman's World.

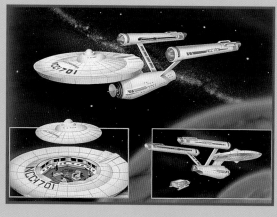

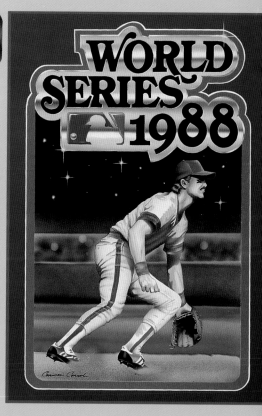

Carmen Console

Illustration and Design Studio

(609) 424-8735

Voorhees, New Jersey

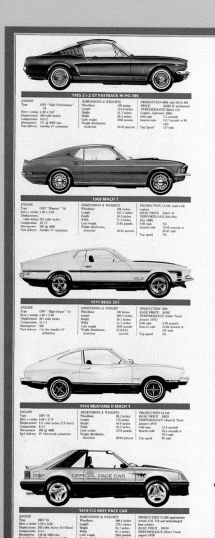

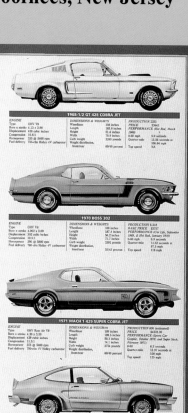

Joe Boddy

406-251-3587

5375 Skyway Dr. • Missoula MT 59801

CLIENTS INCLUDE
Scott Foresman • Houghton Mifflin • Western • Zaner Bloser
Silver Burdett & Ginn • D.C. Heath • Modern Curriculum Press
Sesame Street • Dover • Turtle • Child's Life • Child's Digest
Child's Playmate • Humpty Dumpty • Highlights for Children
Unicorn • Milliken • Revell • Thomas Nelson • D.C. Cook
School Zone • Wolgemuth & Hyatt • Dillon • Santillana
Abbington • Concordia • Standard • Augsburg • Impact

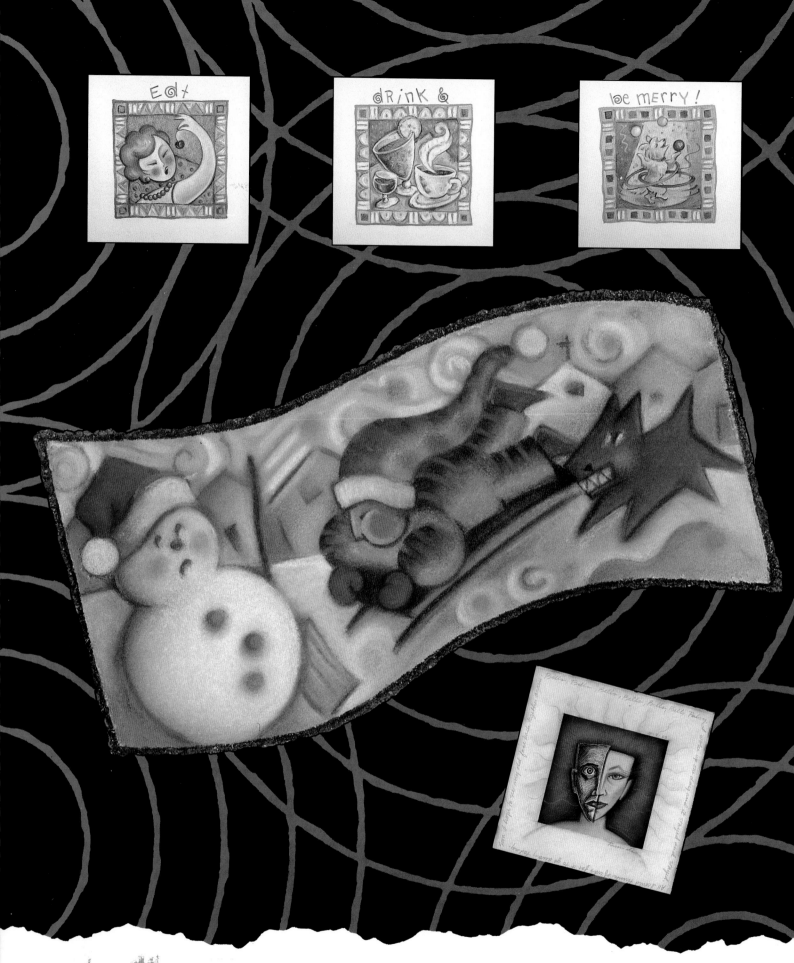

ILLUSTRATION

DESIGN

PAM-ELA HARRELSON

2707 BEECHMONT DRIVE • DALLAS • TEXAS • 75228 • 214-321-6061

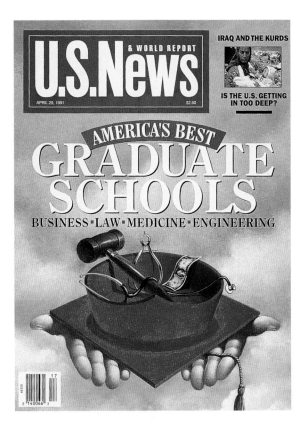

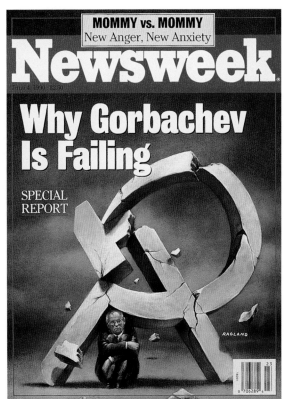

Greg Ragland

GREG RAGLAND ILLUSTRATION
2500 LUCKY JOHN DRIVE
PARK CITY, UT 84060

(801) 645-9232
FAX (801) 645-9309

Clients include: AT&T; B.B.D.O.; Byte Magazine; Book-of-the-Month Club; California Magazine; C.E.O. Brief; Chemical Bank; Chief Executive; Citibank; D Magazine; Financial World; Governing Magazine; GQ; Harper-Collins; J. Walter Thompson; L.A. Times; Lears; Longevity; Lotus Magazine; Manner Vogue; "M" Inc.; Money Magazine; Newsweek; New York Times; New York Woman; Penguin USA; Pocket Books; Psychology Today; Ron Rezek Furniture; Serino, Coyne & Nappi; Seventeen Magazine; Simon & Schuster; Southern Magazine; Sports Illustrated; Siddall, Matus & Coughter; Tampa Bay Life; Texas Monthly; Union Service Employees; U.S. News & World Report; Whittle Communications.

David Levinson

219-D Richfield Terrace
Clifton, New Jersey 07012

(201) 614-1627

E.Fowler

Eric N. Fowler

417 BEATTY STREET
TRENTON, NEW JERSEY 08611

(609) 695-4305

Clients: Harper & Row, Viking/
Penguin, E.P. Dutton, St. Martins Press,
Holt, Reinhart & Winston, The New
York Times, Penthouse, Sports Illus-
trated, Redbook, Condé Nast/The
Traveler, American Express, Pacific
Bell, Foote, Cone & Belding, RCA

Records, IBM, Psychology Today, Ciba-
Geigy, McGraw-Hill, PC Week, Emergency Medicine.

SAM SCALI

ILLUSTRATION   718-859-0814

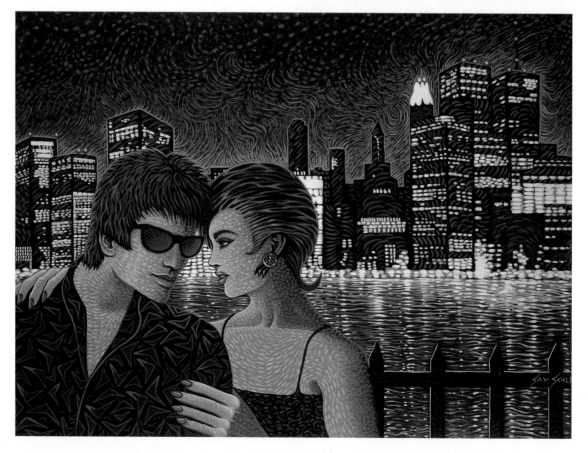

Bob Doughty

BOB DOUGHTY/ILLUSTRATION, ETC.
839 S. BEACON STREET, SUITE 308
SAN PEDRO, CA 90731

(213) 548-3383

PEOPLE

Illustration with emphasis on corporate and commemorative portraits, caricatures, children's likenesses, romantic fantasy. Work accomplished in several media from life or photos.

Clients include: TRW, Rockwell, Bank of America, TransAmerica, Hughes Helicopter, and lots of others nobody's heard of.

AMERICA IS
BUSH'd

Don't let your next camping trip become your...

LAST CRUSADE

USE QUALITY OUTDOOR
GEAR FROM
REI

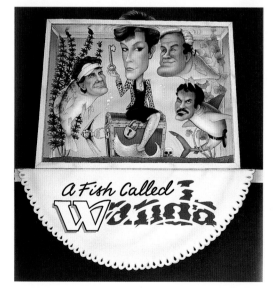

A Fish Called
Wanda

Glen Evans

GLEN EVANS DESIGN & ILLUSTRATION
1444 HONEYHILL DRIVE
WALNUT, CALIFORNIA 91789

(714) 595-5512
FAX & MACINTOSH COMPUTER IN STUDIO.

Clients include: Disney, NBC, Universal
Studios, Stephen J. Cannell Productions, Mobil, Arco, Amway, Knott's
Berry Farm.
Specializing in: Caricature, likenesses,
hand lettering, logo design, corporate
identity.

For: Ad agencies, editorial pages, film
and TV production companies, amuse-
ment parks; movie posters, greeting
cards, books.

Member: Graphic Artists Guild; Society
of Illustrators, Los Angeles

Awards/Shows: Society of Illustrators,
New York; Winterfest, Laguna Beach,
California
On Glen Evans: "His work has person-
ality, flair and style. He's a pleasure to
work with."

—*Linda Cushing, Creative Director, Ad America*

99

Pam Posey

PAM POSEY ILLUSTRATION
2763 COLLEGE BLVD.
OCEANSIDE, CA 92056

(619) 724-3566

Clients have included: Random House, Inc., American Greetings Corp., Troll/ Compass Productions, Macmillan Publishing Co., Sesame Street.
Member: Society of Illustrators, San Diego; Greater San Diego Basset Hound Club.

Media: Graphite, watercolor, gouache, acrylic; R.D.B. (Rural Domestic Bliss)

Travel: Disneyland, Reno, and Downtown San Diego.

Kim Fraley

KIM FRALEY ILLUSTRATION
511 SMILAX ROAD
VISTA, CA 92083

(619) 727-3511

Clients have included: Wadsworth, Journeys, Scripps Memorial Hospital, CBS, HBJ.

Member: Society of Illustrators, San Diego

Media: Colored Pencils, Watercolor, Toned Paper, Graphite, and R.D.B. (Rural Domestic Bliss)

Travel has included: Africa, Australia, New Zealand, England, United States and Disneyland.

Judy Unger

16014 Lahey Street
Granada Hills, CA 91344

(818) 368-2111

Clients include: Bank of America, Borden, Budget Gourmet, Carnation, Celestial Seasonings, Chevron, Conroy Flowers, Crystal Geyser, Dole, Del Monte, General Foods, General Mills, Hallmark, Heinz, Kraft, M&M Mars,

Nabisco, Oscar Mayer, People Magazine, Shasta, Sparkletts McKesson, Visa.

Member Society of Illustrators, Los Angeles. Exhibitor in Illustration West annually since 1982.

Representatives:
San Francisco: Barb Hauser
(415) 339-1885
New York: Penny & Stermer Group
(212) 243-4412

David Scott Meier

DAVID SCOTT MEIER/DESIGN
125 CEDAR WAY
LAGUNA BEACH, CALIFORNIA 92651

(714) 494-4206

DAVID SCOTT MEIER paints finely patterned figures and designs for book illustration, packaging and greeting cards. His mixed-media work is inspired by his encounters with international folk art. His paintings are regularly displayed in his working studio in Laguna Beach and are included in that city's annual juried exhibition. Fast turn-around time.

Published: EL TORITO CORP. (Menu design); CAROLYN BEAN (Greeting cards); PICTURE BOOK STUDIO (Children's books)

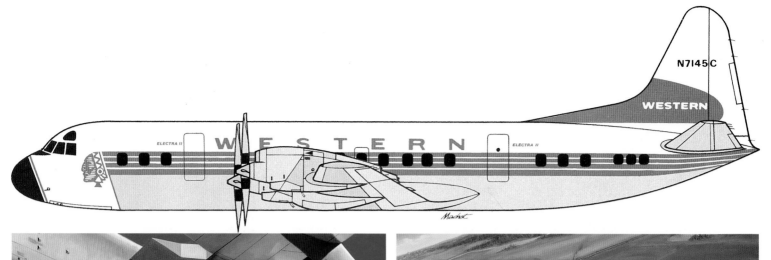

Mike Machat

4426 Deseret Drive
Woodland Hills, CA 91364

(818) 591-9433
Fax (818) 591-9495

Specializing in all aspects of aircraft illustration.

Clients include: AiResearch, Crown Publishing Group, Delta Air Lines, Flying Tigers, Lufthansa, McDonnell Douglas, NASA, National Air & Space Museum, Pan Am, Popular Mechanics,

Reader's Digest, Soaring Society of America, U.S. Air Force.

Organizations: American Society of Aviation Artists, Society of Illustrators of Los Angeles, USAF Documentary Art Program.

Exhibits/Awards: USAF Museum—ASAA Exhibit, 1989; San Diego Aerospace Museum—One Man Show, 1981; National Soaring Museum—Permanent Collection; Illustration West—Best of Category, Corporate; Silver Medal, Technical.

Miguel Angel Camarena

MIGUEL ANGEL
445 W. LEXINGTON DRIVE #5
GLENDALE, CA 91203

(818) 246-8081

Miguel Angel's sensitive portraits capture the spirits, moods, and surroundings of the individuals he portrays. His command of a range of media and techniques—from rich acrylic paints to soft pastel, oils and airbrush—enables him to capture the essence of each subject at a particular moment and time.

Shannon Hogan

715 MARCO PLACE
VENICE, CA 90291

(213) 821-8131

A member of The Society of Illustrators, Shannon Hogan has been a popular Southland illustrator and storyboard/comp artist for the past twelve years. She's represented in all fields by Famous Frames, Inc. (213-558-3325).

Her clients include: McCann Erickson, Saatchi & Saatchi, Max Factor, American Artist Magazine, Carnation, Toyota, NBC, Dole Foods, Lord Dentsu, Grey Advertising, Dailey & Associates, Admarketing, Ogilvy & Mather, Hill/Holliday, Ayer/Tuttle, Sheraton Hotels, Foote, Cone & Belding, J. Walter Thompson, Home Savings of America, Disneyland, Sachs Finley, Paramount Pictures.

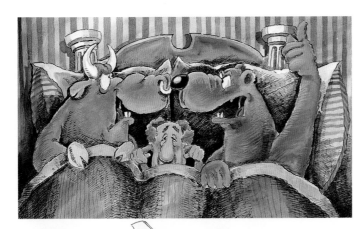

Stan Gorman

STAN GORMAN ART COMMUNICATIONS
185 ESPLANADE
IRVINE, CA 92715

(714) 733-8071
FAX IN STUDIO.

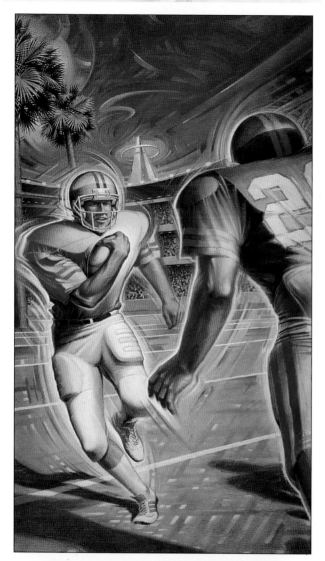

A N D R E von M O R I S S E

212 - 406-21-77   fax 212 - 406-22-78,   92 Reade street, 3 floor   N.Y. N.Y.   10013

Andrea Bolton
1800 State Street #76
South Pasadena, California 91030

(818) 441-0620

Clients include: Reflex, Inc.–Mattel, Disney, Sega Genesis, Warner Bros. International Strategic Marketing—Denneys, Golden Eagle Awards, International Guitar Month.

Premier Promotions—Colgate Palmolive, Mission Foods, Gillette, Pangea, Triple Time, Inc.

C. WINSTON TAYLOR
17008 LISETTE ST.
GRANADA HILLS, CA 91344
818/363-5761

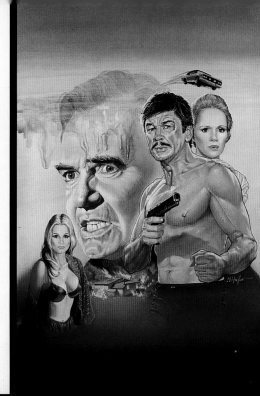

BLACKBIRD FLY

An
Ashley Tyler
Film

Whoopi Goldberg   **Rain Pryor**
Garrett Morris   **Esther Rolle**

Introducing **Jay Brooks** as "Jake" and **Maurice Prince** as "Miss Sarah" Based upon the Short Story "Time To Care" by **Ashley Tyler & Holle Robertson**
Director of Photography **Mario Di Leo** Additional Photography **John Simmons** Editor **Gina Gallo** Supervising Sound Editor **Thierry Couturier**
Executive Music Producer **Joel Moss** Original Music Score **Oscar Castro-Neves** Casting Director **Pamela Goodlow** Production Designer **Harold Michelson**
"**Let The Children Sing**" words and music by **Joel Moss & Steve Deutsch** performed by **Kim Carnes** and **The McCrary Family**
Executive Producer **Thomas McGovern** Associate Producers **Pamela Goodlow, Gregory Alexander, Alana Rothstein**
Producer **Holle Robertson** Written, Produced and Directed by **Ashley Tyler**

ADVENTURE AIRLINES

M.K. Montgomery

1150 Pine Tree Lane
Sebastopol, CA 95472

(707) 829-2135

Los Angeles Society of Illustrators
San Francisco Society of Illustrators

Jude Maceren

92 KOSSUTH STREET
PISCATAWAY, NEW JERSEY 08854

(908) 752-5931
FAX (908) 752-5931

A style that suits your needs. Excellent figure and creative illustrations. Produced to meet your budget and deadline. Fast and dependable. Call for details.

Member Graphic Artists Guild

© Jude Maceren 1990

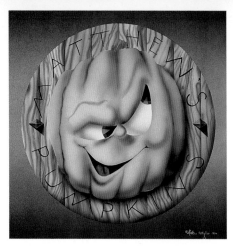

Matthew C. Gallagher
1 OLD MANOR ROAD
HOLMDEL, NJ 07733

(908) 888-3953

Graduated from The University of the Arts with a B.F.A. in Illustration. Specializing in airbrush illustration with subjects ranging from portraits and humorous illustrations, to illustrative logos.

Clients have included: MTV, Nickelodeon, VH-1, Gitano Jeans, Granite Capital Corporation, Ripley's Believe It Or Not, and The Gap.

If you wish to see my portfolio, please call me.

Member of the Graphic Artists Guild.

Peter Bianco

ILLUSTRATOR
BiancoMarchilonis Design
348 Manning Street
Needham, MA 02192

Tel/Fax (617) 444-9077

Clients: AT&T, Animal Rescue League of Boston, Banyan Systems Corporation, Curriculum Associates, Danforth Museum of Art, Dun & Bradstreet Software, Inc., Houghton Mifflin, Massachusetts Financial Services, Inc., MicroAmerica Corporation, New York Woman Magazine, WCVB, Channel 5.

Memberships: AIGA, GAG

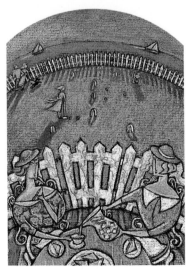

Cynthia Carrozza

CYNTHIA CARROZZA ILLUSTRATION
343 MARLBOROUGH STREET
BOSTON, MA 02116

(617) 437-7428
FAX (617) 859-7865

Clients: Boston Globe, Castle Hill Foundation, Changing Times, Christian Science Monitor, Connoisseur, DC Heath, Educational Resource Institute, Four Seasons Hotel, GK Hall, Governing, George Washington University, Houghton Mifflin, Marshall's, National Association of Executive Females, News 3X/400 (IBM), Northeastern University, Peachtree Publishing, Powell Adams & Rinehart (Ogilvy & Mather), Run (Commodore), Seventeen, Silver Burdett & Ginn, Teen.

Media: Pastels, scratchboard.

Member Graphic Artists Guild.

Lonni Sue Johnson

LONNI SUE JOHNSON INC.
310 WEST 72 STREET, PH #3
NEW YORK, NY 10023

(212) 873-7749
(203) 355-9359

Parents Magazine, Lotus Development
Corp., The Baltimore Sun, Corning
Glass, Arthur Anderson, The Museum
of Modern Art, The Boston Globe, The
New Yorker, Champion International,
Postgraduate Medicine, Atheneum,
HarperCollins, The New York Times,

Citibank, Roher Pharmaceuticals,
Bozell Omaha, Digital, Southwestern
Bell, Bantam Books, Grove
Weidenfeld.

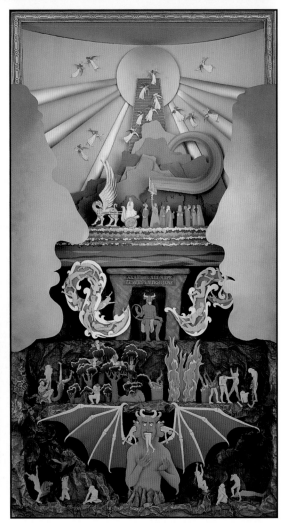

Ellen Rixford

ELLEN RIXFORD STUDIO
308 WEST 97TH STREET, APT. 71
NEW YORK, NY 10025

(212) 865-5686

Award-winning, internationally known dimensional illustration in paper, wood, fabric, plastics, and God knows what else—plus studio photography. Clients include: Business Week, Fortune, Newsweek, NBC, DDB Needham, J. Walter Thompson, O & M, Saatchi & Saatchi, Sudler & Hennessey, Y & R, General Foods, McNeil/Lehrer.
The Pictures: Left: Peaceable Kingdom (salute to Edward Hicks), Good Housekeeping Magazine. Right: Palladio's Church of the Redentore; paper, wood, and foam sculpture: Gucci's Christmas windows. Right: Dante's Divine Comedy; paper, board and foam sculpture: Gucci's Christmas windows. Left: Zeus and Ganymede on Mt. Olympus reviewing Best and Worst Annual Reports, 1989; Chief Executive Magazine, in soft sculpture with multimedia landscape.

John Paul Genzo

JOHN PAUL GENZO ILLUSTRATION
802 RAVENS CREST DRIVE
PLAINSBORO, NEW JERSEY 08536

(609) 275-5601
FAX (609) 799-8707

Clients include: American Journal of Nursing, Carol & Graff Publishing, Chelsea House Publishing, Citibank, Digital Computers, Fidelity Investments, Harcourt, Brace, Jovanovich Publications, HarperCollins Publishing, Hospital Practice Publishing Company, Inter-Governmental Philatelic Corporation, Ketchum Advertising, Marketing Communication Systems Inc., McGraw-Hill, National Review Magazine, The New Republic Magazine, Penguin Books Canada, Pennsylvania Hospital, Public Relations Journal, Saint Michael's Medical Center, Scholastic Books, Sea World, G.D. Searle & Company, Springhouse Corporation, Sunkist, World Health Communications, Inc.

Member Graphic Artists Guild

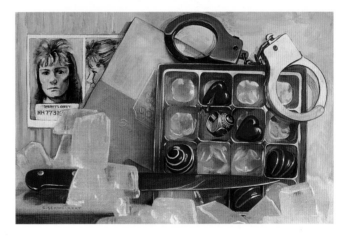

Carol Schweigert

791 TREMONT STREET
BOSTON, MA 02118

(617) 262-8909

Illustration for the editorial, publishing
and corporate client.

Top—A John Glenn Triptych.
Bottom—A Mary Shelley Portrait, and
Love and Murder in New Hampshire.

Susan Swan

83 Saugatuck Avenue
Westport, CT 06880

(203) 226-9104
Fax (203) 454-7956

Clients: Publisher's Weekly Magazine; Chemical Bank; CMP Publications; Harcourt Brace Jovanovich; Scholastic; Houghton Mifflin Company; Holt Rinehart Winston; Bantam Doubleday Dell; Silver Burdett and Ginn; Putnam; Macmillan/McGraw-Hill; Walker and Company; Scott Foresman and Company; Harper and Row; Children's Television Workshop.

See also: The Creative Illustration Book 1992; Corporate Showcase Vol. 10; Graphic Artists Guild Directory #5, 6 and 8.

Member Graphic Artists Guild

Lou Carbone

602 PARK AVENUE #10
HOBOKEN, NJ 07030

(201) 656-6008

Clients include: Adweek, AT&T, Billboard, Book-of-the-Month Club, Con Edison, Crown, Della Femina McNamee WCRS Inc., Macmillan, McCall's, McGraw-Hill, National Lampoon, New York Magazine, NYNEX, Panasonic, Poppe Tyson, Scholastic, South Central Bell, St. Martins, Viking, Waldenbooks.

Member: Graphic Artists Guild, Society of Illustrators

Also see: Communication Arts Illustration Annual 1988; Creative Illustration, Volume 2; American Showcase (illustration).

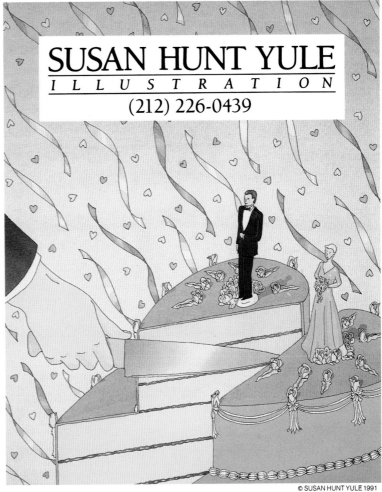

SUSAN HUNT YULE
I L L U S T R A T I O N
(212) 226-0439

© SUSAN HUNT YULE 1991

Alfred Ramage

SILENT SOUNDS STUDIO
5 IRWIN STREET
WINTHROP, MA 02152

(617) 846-5955
FAX IN STUDIO

Member Graphic Artists Guild

Also see: *Graphic Artists Guild's Directory of Illustration 5, 6, 7.*
"Conceptual imagination, will travel."
Media: Oil, ink, watercolor, collage, colored pencil, mixed.

Expertise: Editorial, book cover, advertising, 3D action premiums, graphics, exhibit design.

CHiD

55 Desmond Avenue
Bronxville, NY 10708

Phone/Fax (914) 793-5220

To describe Chid is as difficult as whistling Beethoven's Fifth with a mouthful of crackers. Whether one has intentions of slaying dragons or sledding into a tree, Chid is guaranteed to be suitable for your needs. Chid's style is quick, bold, and versatile in order to keep up with the world's ever changing trends as well as the demanding needs of clients.

Portfolio and client list available on request.

Work also appears in the Graphic Artists Guild Directory #6 and #7.

Member Graphic Artists Guild.

Dorothy Leech
1024 Avenue of the Americas
New York, New York 10018

(212) 354-6641
Fax (212) 840-9452

Clients: Times Books/Random House, Marboro Books, Chelsea House Publishers, Scholastic, Hearst Magazines, New York *Times,* New York *Daily News,* Liz Claiborne, Guess, AT&T, IBM, Marine Midland Bank, Scott Paper Company, DMB&B Advertising.

For other samples, also see The Creative Illustration Book 1992, RSVP #14 and RSVP #17.

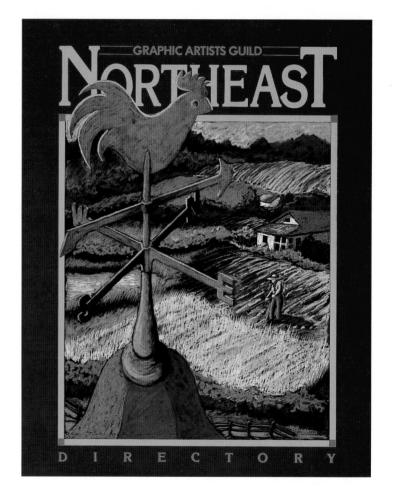

GRAPHIC ARTISTS GUILD

NORTHEAST

DIRECTORY

Sophia Latto

723 PRESIDENT STREET
BROOKLYN, NEW YORK 11215

(718) 789-1980

Client List: American Banker, American Express, American Management Association, Doubleday, Cardiology News, Cooper-Hewitt Museum, Hudson River Museum, Laguna Sportswear, Lynch, Jones & Ryan, Medical Communique, New York City Transit Authority, Resortworks, The Salvation Army.

Member: Graphic Artists Guild, Brooklyn Communication Arts Professionals and Society of Illustrators.

Gretchen Geser

58 Bank Street
New York, NY 10014

(212) 366-1404

Clients include: VARBusiness magazine, New Age Journal, Travel Holiday magazine, Bostonia and Restaurant Business magazine.

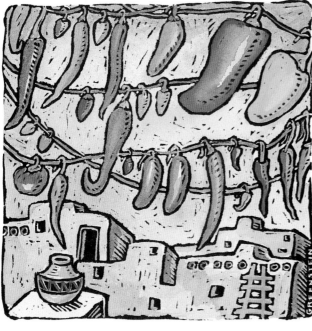

Susan Greenstein

4915 Surf Avenue
Brooklyn, New York 11224

(718) 373-4475

- New Woman Magazine
- Audio Magazine
- John Wiley & Sons Publishing
- Cornell University
- Travel & Leisure Magazine
- American Booksellers Association

- Global Finance Magazine
- Walker & Co. Publishing
- Brooklyn AIDS Task Force
- Muscular Dystrophy Association
- Applause Magazine
- Deutsch Design

- Continental Insurance
- Changing Times Magazine
- McGraw-Hill, Inc.
- Ronn Campisi Design
- Lotus
- The Brooklyn Children's Museum

Garison Weiland

(617) 983-9251

To view more work see Directory of Illustration #6, and American Showcase #15.

L E W I S

184 ST. JOHNS PLACE

BROOKLYN, NY 11217

718   857 - 3406

FAX: 398 - 3788

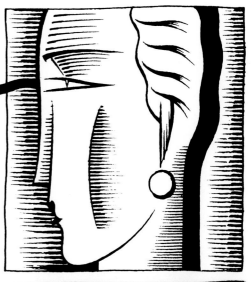

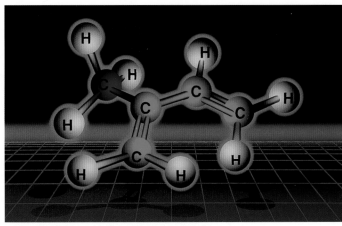

Gary Ferster

57 WEST END AVENUE

LONG BRANCH, NJ 07740

(908) 229-5774

Macintosh® Computer Illustration.

Member Graphic Artists Guild.

132

Jack Barrett
88 Dartmouth Street
Portland, ME 04103

(207) 772-3992
Fax (207) 774-5956

Illustration
Custom Type

Member:
• Graphic Artists Guild
• Art Directors Club
• Environmental Defense Fund
• Trout Unlimited
• World Wildlife Fund
• Southern Maine Blues Society

Instructor:
• Portland School of Art
• Portland Adult Community Education

© Jack Barrett 1991

Frederick H. Carlson

F. Carlson Illustration
118 Monticello Drive
Monroeville, PA 15146-4837

(412) 856-0982
Fax (412) 856-0983

Clients include: McDonald's Corporation, USX Corporation, National Science Foundation, *New York Times, Saturday Evening Post, National Review,* Canadian Club, Standard Oil of Ohio, Heinz, Rockwell International, Zurn Industries, Westinghouse, McGraw-Hill, *Baltimore Sun,* Shanachie Recordings. Exhibitions have included: New York, Switzerland, Quebec. Executive Committee of the Graphic Artists Guild. Overnight portfolio delivery. Pictured above: Top—*Pittsburgh Magazine* (AD: Mike Maskarinec). Bottom— *Saturday Evening Post* (AD: Chris Wilhoite).

Tom Huffman

130 West 47th Street, Apt. 6A
New York, NY 10036

(212) 819-0211
Fax available.

CALLING PLANET MIRTH . . . CALLING PLANET MIRTH . . . DO YOU READ ME? A celestial body of heavenly ideas has been spotted illuminating the sky. They are waiting to be claimed by anyone who needs a spark of humor to launch a galaxy of gags. Count them down in black or white or shoot for the stars in luminous color.

5 . . . 4 . . . 3 . . . 2 . . . 1—BLAST OFF! Star clients include: AC&R Advertising ★ AT&T ★ Bozell, Inc. ★ Chiat/Day/ Mojo ★ Cosmopolitan ★ Esquire ★ Greenwillow Press ★ Grey Advertising ★ HBO ★ Houghton Mifflin ★ Kallir Philips, Ross, Inc. ★ Macy's ★ McGraw-Hill ★ Merrill Lynch ★ Ogilvy and Mather ★ Pfizer ★ Saatchi and Saatchi DFS Compton ★ Sudler and Hennessey, Inc. ★ UNICEF ★ Woman's Day ★ Young and Rubicam.

RECKLESS

BY CRAIG LUCAS
DIRECTED BY MAUREEN HEFFERNAN
DECEMBER 28–FEBRUARY 4 ★ 321-9800

Pittsburgh Public Theater

Ilene Winn-Lederer

986 LILAC STREET
PITTSBURGH, PA 15217

(412) 421-8668
FAX IN STUDIO

Clients include: McDonald's Corporation; Westinghouse Electric Corporation; Holiday Inn Corporation; TWA; MGM Studios, Inc.; Portal Publications; Recycled Paper Products, Inc.; Inland Steel Corp.; Van Nostrand, Reinhold Publishers; Doubleday & Co. Publishers; Simon & Schuster, Publishers; Physicians For The Prevention of Nuclear War; The American Medical Women's Association; The Pittsburgh Public Theater Corporation; Ketchum Communications, Inc.; Washington & Jefferson College; Carnegie-Mellon University; Pittsburgh Magazine/WQED-TV-FM; Pitt Magazine; University of Pittsburgh; The Pittsburgh Civic Light Opera; Neutrogena, Inc.; Postal Instant Press, Inc.
Professional Associations: Graphic Artists Guild, Illustration Faculty/College of Fine Arts, Carnegie-Mellon University
Publications: Print Magazine, Regional Design Annual, 1986, pp. 223/241.

Frances Middendorf
337 East 22nd Street #2
New York, New York 10010

(212) 473-3586

Clients (partial list): New York Times, Gralla Publications, American Laywer Media, American Journal of Nursing, East West Journal, Insurance Review Magazine, Advantage Advertising, The Gift Wrap Company, Flying Magazine, North Star Records and Rhode Island Monthly.

Member of the Graphic Artists Guild.

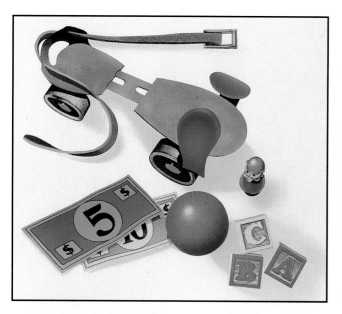

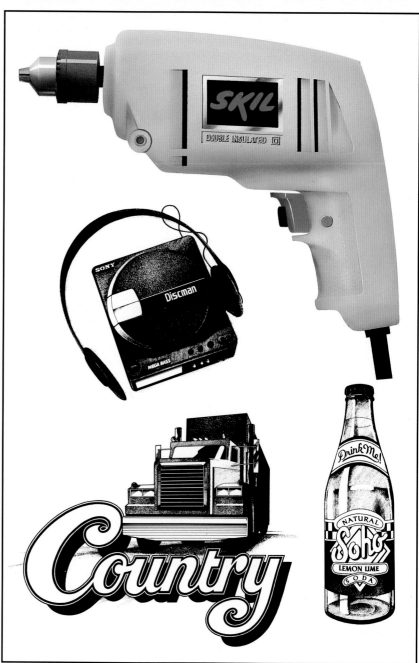

Errico Gregory

ERRICO GREGORY ILLUSTRATION
32 MONROE STREET
NEW YORK, NEW YORK 10002

(212) 233-2589

- Advertising and Editorial Illustration
- Illustration for Comps and Storyboards
- Fine Hand Lettering

Member Graphic Artists Guild

© Errico Gregory 1991

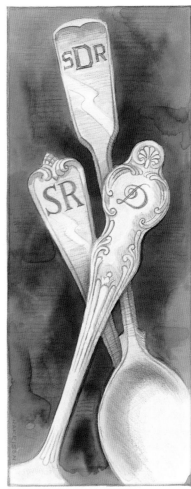

Hugh Harrison

314 Payonia Avenue
Jersey City, NJ 07302

(201) 798-6086

Pen and ink, colored pencils and
watercolor.

Member Graphic Artists Guild

See also Graphic Artists Guild
Directory of Illustration #7

JEFF SEAVER

130 W 24TH ST #4B NY, NY 10011-1906 FAX 212/255-3823 PHONE 212/741-2279

Dorothea Sierra

1 FITCHBURG STREET, #C421
SOMERVILLE, MA 02143

PHONE & FAX (617) 625-8070

Graphic illustration in gouache, ink, cut paper, and pattern. Specializing in cultural and environmental work developed through research, travels and studies in animal, aquatic, botanical and various cultural ethnic groups patterning and coloration. Work in publishing (books, covers and interiors) and consultant in conceptual development through graphics, art and color coordination. Additional work for magazines, corporations, exhibit art, posters and greeting cards. Awards: Boston Bookbuilders Assoc./covers and interior illustration; Marketing/ posters. Member: Brickbottom Artists Assoc., Board of Directors; Boston Computer Society; Graphic Artists Guild; Surface Design Assoc.

Anna Veltfort

16 West 86 Street, #B
New York, NY 10024

(212) 877-0430

Gary Symington

Middle Street Studios
47 Middle Street
Portland, ME 04101

(207) 774-4977
Fax (207) 774-5956

Clients include: L.L. Bean, McDonald's, Blue Cross, Paine Webber, Teledyne Electronics, Fairchild Schlumberger, Educational Insights (Los Angeles), Oakhurst, Country Kitchen Bread, IDEXX, Family Planning Association, Ventrex, Peoples Heritage Bank, Northern Utilities, Maine Tourism, Northeastern Log Homes, United Publications, Craftsman Book Co., Bay State Gas.

Awards: Society of Illustrators of Los Angeles—Merit Award
Strathmore Paper Graphics Gallery

Member Graphic Artists Guild

Plato Taleporos

333 East 23rd Street
New York, NY 10010

(212) 689-3138
Fax in studio

Shown above:
Center: New York Newsday (spread)
"Passport to Off-Broadway"

Corners, clockwise from upper left:
1. Industry Week "Care to Share"
2. People Weekly "Terms of
   Bombardment"
3. YM "Why They Don't Call"
4. NY Newsday (promotional mailer)

Clients include: Adweek Promote;
Baltimore Sun; Bozell, Jacobs, Kenyon
& Eckhardt; Business Week; Cosmo-
politan; Financial World; Governing;
Money; New York Life Insurance; New
York Times; Runners World; Scholastic;
Ski; Travel & Leisure; Workman Press.

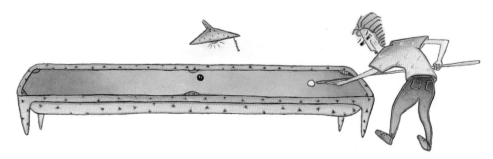

**Andrea Faraclas
Jennison**
227 Christopher Columbus Dr., #335 B
Jersey City, NJ 07302

(201) 433-3459

Clients include:
ACP Observer, Boston College, Boston
Globe, City News, Golf Shop Opera-
tions, Lotus, Network World, New
England Business Magazine, Run
Magazine.

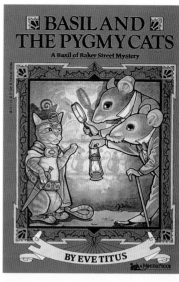

Judith Sutton

239 Dean Street
Brooklyn, New York 11217

(718) 834-8851

146

Our
Yearbox
for
1991

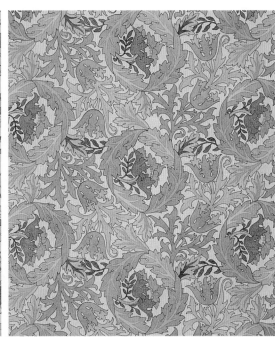

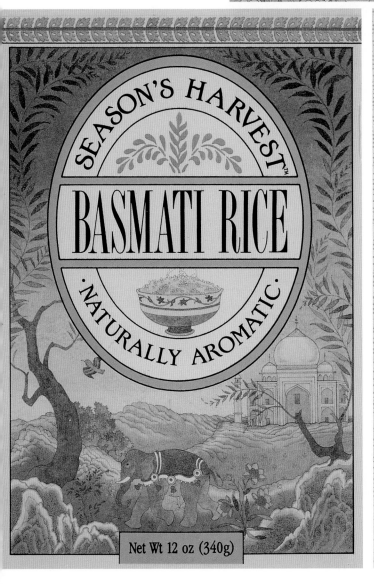

SEASON'S HARVEST™

BASMATI RICE

NATURALLY AROMATIC.

Net Wt 12 oz (340g)

a
Baby
KEEPBOX™
for

Judith Sutton

239 Dean Street
Brooklyn, New York 11217

(718) 834-8851

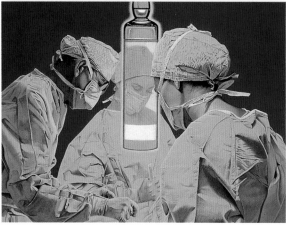

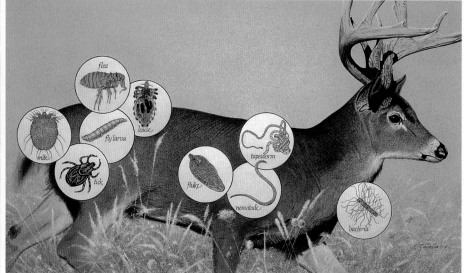

Sal Catalano

114 Boyce Place
Ridgewood, NJ 07450

(201) 447-5318

Clients include:
National Aububon Society; Ciba Geigy; American Motors; CBS; NBC; Coca-Cola; General Foods; N.Y. Zoological Society; Canada Dry; ABC; Time/Life; Pepsi-Cola; Citibank; Travenol; U.S. Government; Upjohn; Lederle; Pfizer; Winthrop; Burger King; IBM; DuPont; United Artists; Sony; Panasonic; Borden; McGraw/Hill; RCA; TWA; McNeil; Squibb; Wyeth; Sterling; American Distillers; N.J. Bell; Paramount Studios; Merck; The Rockefeller Group; Paine Webber; Avon Books; HarperCollins; National Wildlife Federation; *Reader's Digest;* American Museum of Natural History; Exxon; Becton Dickinson; *Field & Stream; TV Guide; Smithsonian, The New Yorker; N.Y. Times.*

Blake Thornton

19235 CARRIGER ROAD
SONOMA, CA 95476

(707) 935-9716
FAX (707) 935-3687

Hi! My service-oriented studio provides a wide range of quality-minded art directors, designers and other professionals with creative illustration and design for advertising, corporate, editorial, publishing, film and packaging that is unique and effective . . . on time with spotless execution.

I can do the same for you!

PacBell; Dole; Williams-Sonoma; The Movie Channel; Portal Publications; Publish!; Oddzon Toys; The Seattle Mariners; McDonald's; DMB&B/Chi-Chi's; Chevron

SUSAN DETRICH · ILLUSTRATION

SUSAN DETRICH • 253 Baltic Street • Brooklyn New York 11201 • 718-237-9174

For more work see the Graphic Artists Guild's Directory of Illustration 5, 6, the Creative Illustration Book 1991 & RSVP 16, 17

Michael McGurl

14 Garbosa Road
Santa Fe, NM 87505

(505) 986-5889
Fax in studio.

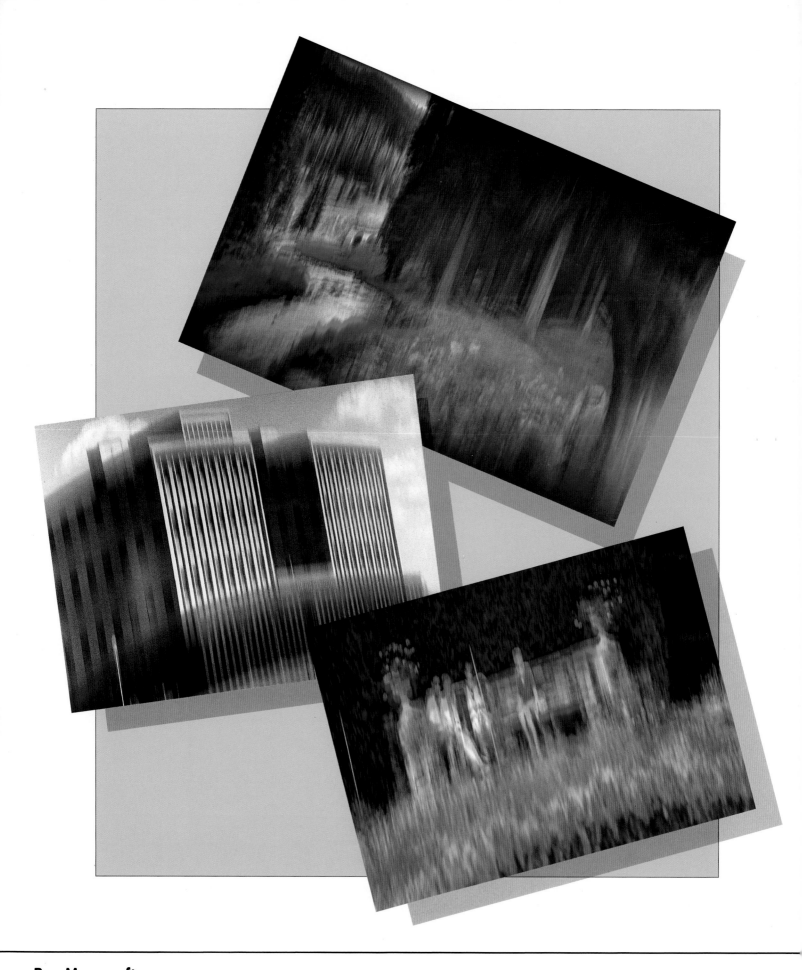

Ron Morecraft

97 Morris Avenue
Denville, NJ 07834

(201) 625-5752
Fax in studio (201) 586-1046

Member Graphic Artists Guild

Special Effects Photography, large selection of stock images.

To view more work: American Showcase 4, 9, 10.

Clients include: ABC, MTV, CBS Records, AT&T, Business Week, Paramount Pictures, Parke-Davis, Omni, Grey Advertising, Revlon, Elizabeth Arden, Mazda.

Judith DuFour Love

AM Studios
68 Agassiz Avenue
Belmont, MA 02178

(617) 484-8023

Clients: D.C. Heath; Houghton Mifflin;
Silver, Burdett and Ginn; Kirchoff
Wohlberg, Inc.; The Boston Globe;
Digital Review; Ingalls, Quinn and
Johnson; Continental Cablevision;
Bank of Boston; New England
Aquarium.

Toby Williams

84 FRANKLIN STREET
WATERTOWN, MA 02172

©TOBY WILLIAMS, 1991

Clients include:
Boston University
D.C. Heath
Houghton Mifflin
Medical Economics, Inc.

Presbyterian Medical Center/Philadelphia
Silver Burdett & Ginn

Marilyn Cathcart

(314)862-2644

6933 COLUMBIA AVENUE
ST. LOUIS, MO 63130

©MARILYN CATHCART, 1991

Clients include:
Cahners Publishing
Christian Science Monitor
CW Communications
Doubleday

Fidelity Investments
John Hancock Insurance
St. Louis Magazine
St. Louis Post-Dispatch

Joni Levy Liberman

(617)986-4657

14 HILL PARK TERRACE
RANDOLPH, MA 02368

©JONI LEVY LIBERMAN, 1991

Clients include:
The Boston Globe
Computerworld
The Detroit News
G.K. Hall/Macmillan

Hewlett Packard
Houghton Mifflin
The Washington Post
WGBH

Suzette Barbier

(617)739-2822

7 DEVOTION STREET, #3
BROOKLINE, MA 02146

FAX (617)734-8827

©SUZETTE BARBIER, 1991

Clients include:
The Boston Globe
General Motors
The Hartford Courant
Houghton Mifflin

IBM
Lotus
USA Today
WGBH Radio
Whittle Communications

Elizabeth Stubbs (617)646-0785

27 WYMAN STREET
ARLINGTON, MA 02174

©ELIZABETH STUBBS, 1991

Clients include:
The Baltimore Sun
The Boston Globe
Cahners Publishing
CFO Magazine

C.W. Publishing
The Hartford Courant
McGraw-Hill
Simon & Schuster

STUDIOS

Mary Newell DePalma (617)327-6241

©Newell '92

45 BRADFIELD AVENUE
BOSTON, MA 02131

©MARY NEWELL DEPALMA, 1991

Pen and ink or colored pencil
illustration with an emphasis
on pattern and texture

STUDIOS

Julia Talcott

AM STUDIOS
38 LINDEN STREET #3
BROOKLINE, MA 02146

(617) 232-7306
FAX IN STUDIO

Clockwise from left:
Boston Globe
Personal Work
Lotus
Digital

MUSIC TELEVISION

YOU ARE HERE

Dan V. Romer

125 PROSPECT PARK WEST, #2A
BROOKLY, NY 11215

(718) 965-2524

Illuminated bus shelter poster
46" x 67"

See also: *Graphic Artists Guild Directory of Illustration 5, 6, 7* for client lists

DEAN FLEMING

818·795·4636

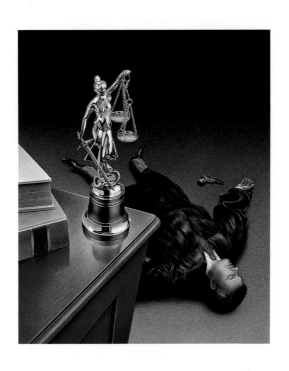

J-DAZE 1990

ICON graphics INC.

Icon Graphics Inc
34 Elton Street
Rochester, New York 14607

(716) 271-7020
FAX (716) 271-7029

Graphic illustration, traditional or electronic.
Call Keith or Steve and ask about our services.
Illustrations can be provided as production film.

Icon Graphics Inc
34 Elton Street
Rochester, New York 14607

(716) 271-7020
FAX (716) 271-7029

ICON
graphics
INC.

Graphic illustration, traditional or electronic.
Call Keith or Steve and ask about our services.
Illustrations can be provided as production film.

Barbara Rhodes

BARBARA RHODES ILLUSTRATION
2730 ARIANE DRIVE #63
SAN DIEGO, CALIFORNIA 92117

(619) 270-5010

Loose watercolor and/or pencil illustration featuring people, fashion, sports, landscape, product.

Clients include:
American Dairy Council, American Red Cross, CBS, Culbertson Winery, *Dance* *Aerobics* Magazine, D.H. Technology, Golden Door Spa, Harcourt Brace Jovanovich, Inc., J.C. Penney, Kyocera International Inc., La Valencia Hotel, New American Library, New Mexico Educators, Ordmark Development Company, Pacific Eyes & T's, Petite Sophisticate, Inc., Scripps Memorial Hospital, Woman's World

Member: Society of Illustrators, San Diego; Graphic Artists Guild

162

Richard Smyth
AIRBRUSH ARTS INC.
1235 GLENVIEW ROAD
GLENVIEW, IL 60025

PHONE & FAX (708) 998-8345

Airbrush, watercolor, pen & ink,
gouache, computer illustration; color,
b/w retouching, both conventional
and computer.

Clients: Scott Foresman Co., The
Quarasan Group, Anixter Inc., Coca-
Cola/Great America, Zylke & Assoc.
Inc., The Goldsholl Group.

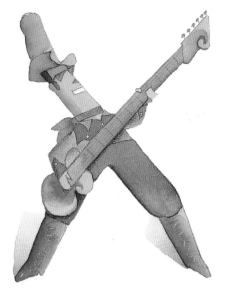

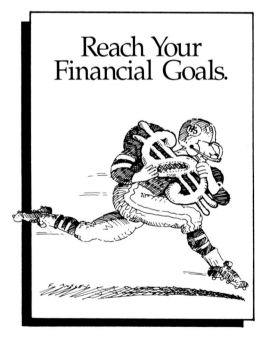

Reach Your Financial Goals.

Two CDs worth their wait.

Improve Your Balance.

Frank Ansley

FRANK ANSLEY/ILLUSTRATION
(415) 989-9614 STUDIO & FAX
(510) 527-1098 HOME

Represented by
Corey Graham
Pier 33 North
San Francisco, CA 94111
(415) 956-4750
FAX (415) 391-6104

BILL GIBBONS
ILLUSTRATION

368 BROADWAY NO 203, NEW YORK, N.Y. 10013   (212) 227-0039

Duke

Marduk A. Sayad

Humorist/Cartoonist
2748 Gamble Court
Hayward, CA 94542

Phone   510 581 4109
FAX   510 581 2569

Fiche-ing tackle.

Zytron has everything for micro-fiche: Readers. Reader/Printers. Chemistry and film. Office micro-filming systems. Storage systems. And all kinds of supplies. From more than 100 manufacturers. As one of the world's largest users, we know our products. We do our own quality testing. And we're installation and maintenance experts, too. Seeking one source for all your fiche needs? You're off the hook now.

Zytron
a company of
The Dun & Bradstreet Corporation

We won't make you feel like a small fiche in a big pond.

We're one of the largest in our business. But we'll never make you feel small. Whether you come to us for computer output microfilm or simple microfilm processing, high-quality laser printing or financial statement printing and mailing services, our unique computerized production control system keeps every job on track—and treats every customer like the biggest in the pond. Call for details.

Zytron
a company of
The Dun & Bradstreet Corporation

Nobody serves fiche the way we do.

Not even you. That's why more and more companies are switching from in-house computer output microfiche processing to Zytron. They thought they'd be better off in-house. But the actual case histories blew the lid off some expensive myths. We lower costs, get jobs done faster, improve quality—and even provide more control over scheduling. Call for a dramatic presentation.

Zytron
a company of
The Dun & Bradstreet Corporation

Fresh fiche daily.

Our fleet of bonded couriers is ready to serve you 24 hours a day, seven days a week. And we don't say "fleet" for nothing. At Zytron, we're quick. Whether you come to us for computer output microfilm or simple microfilm processing, high-quality laser printing, financial statement printing and mailing services, or our complete line of micrographics supplies—expect fast service. Or we'll expect a stink.

Zytron
a company of
The Dun & Bradstreet Corporation

Hiroko

67-12 Yellowstone Blvd.
Forest Hills, New York 11375

Phone & Fax (718) 896-2712

Clients: Avon Books, Bantam Books, Ballantine Books, Berkley Publishing Co., Bill Publication, Book-of-the-Month Club, CBS Records, Chief Executive Magazine, Discover Magazine, Doubleday & Co., Crown—Division of Random House, Financial World, Forbes Magazine, Fortune Magazine, Mobil Co., The New York Times, Penthouse Magazine, Pocket Books, RCA Records, Simon & Schuster Inc., Sieber & McIntyre, Triangle Publications, Young & Rubicam, Warner Books.

Andrew Shachat
P.O. Box 1767
Soquel, California 95073

(408) 475-7544

Client list: Boston Globe, Business Week, Encyclopedia Brittanica, Dial Books, California Magazine, Harcourt Brace Jovanovich, Houghton Mifflin, Lotus, Money, National Lampoon, New Age, New York Times, PC World, PC Computing, Progressive, Psychology Today, Scholastic, Stereo Review, Travel and Leisure, Washington Post, Whittle Communications.

AWARDS: Print's Regional Design Annual, Society of Illustrators, Society of Publication Designers.

Children's Books: "You Can't Catch Me" 1986, "Mommy Doesn't Know My Name" 1990, "The Simple People" 1992.

Dick Cole

66 Broadway
San Francisco, CA 94111

(415) 986-8163

Represented in Los Angeles
by Ann Koeffler
(213) 957-2327

Watercolorist: Food, still life, portrait,
architectural, landscape and product
illustration.

Does not do windows.

M E R Y L
TREATNER
239 Monroe Street Philadelphia, Pennsylvania (215)627-2297

TREATNER

M E R Y L

TREATNER

239 Monroe Street Philadelphia, Pennsylvania (215)627-2297

Steve Gray

1437 A 12TH STREET
MANHATTAN BEACH, CA 90266

(310) 546-2188

Selected client list: AT&T, Coca-Cola, Warner Brothers, Lorimar Films, Fox Broadcasting, Disney Films, Canon, American Express, TRW, First Interstate Bank, Pacific Mutual, Knott's Berry Farm, Century 21 Realty, Sea World, Reader's Digest, General Mills, McDonald's, Sizzler, Pizza Hut, Domino's Pizza, I-Hop, Carl's Jr., Host International, Bacardi Rum, K Swiss, Crazy Shirts Hawaii, Coors, Baskin-Robbins.

Maurice P. Dogué

Maurice P. Dogué

44-55 KISSENA BOULEVARD
FLUSHING, NEW YORK 11355

(718) 358-4685

Graphic Artists Guild member.

All images copyrighted Maurice P. Dogué.

Description: Excellent black and white and color pencil.

Expertise: Musical, Editorial, Real People.

Philosophy: Discover the essential rhythm that makes the most basic shapes exciting.

© Maurice P. Dogué

Jerry Russell Blank

THE BLANK COMPANY
1048 LINCOLN AVENUE
SAN JOSE, CALIFORNIA 95125

(408) 289-9095
FAX (408) 289-8532

Jerry Russell Blank

THE BLANK COMPANY
1048 LINCOLN AVENUE
SAN JOSE, CALIFORNIA 95125

(408) 289-9095
FAX (408) 289-8532

SMITH & JONES

THERESA SMITH

P.O.B. 1932

TUCSON, AZ

85702

602-623-3124

Clients Include:

RCA Records

Tucson Guide Magazine

San Francisco Magazine

Arizona Daily Star

Delphi Press

Harbinger House Books

CATHERINE JONES

P.O.B. 6309

SANTA FE, NM

87502

602-986-9069

Clients Include:

Sage Magazine

Santa Fe Symphony

The Reporter

Go Design

Western Edge

Peter Lautenslager
1289 PARK AVENUE
ROCHESTER, NEW YORK 14610

(716) 425-7870

Specializing in aviation illustration.

Paintings included in the permanent
collection of the Smithsonian Air and
Space Museum and the United States
Air Force art collection. Flight qualified
member of the Air Force Art Program.

Art Glazer
2 James Road
Mt. Kisco, NY 10549

(914) 666-4554

Andrea Baruffi
341 Hudson Terrace
Piermont, NY 10968

(914) 359-9542
Fax available.

Cathy Diefendorf

Represented by Gwen Goldstein
50 Fuller Brook Rd. • Wellesley, MA 02181 • 617-235-8658

Susan Spellman

Represented by Gwen Goldstein
50 Fuller Brook Rd. • Wellesley, MA 02181 • 617-235-8658

ARTISTS' REPRESENTATIVE

GWEN GOLDSTEIN

Gwen Goldstein represents professional illustrators catering to the needs of advertising and book publishing. Call today to receive a complete listing of illustrators and the wide variety of styles from cartoon to photo realism offered to handle your special needs. Fax available.

50 Fuller Brook Rd. • Wellesley, MA 02181 • 6 1 7 • 2 3 5 • 8 6 5 8

Lane Gregory

Represented by Gwen Goldstein
50 Fuller Brook Rd. • Wellesley, MA 02181 • 617-235-8658

COMMISSIONED BY: EPCOT CENTER/DISNEYWORLD

Gary Torrisi

Represented by Gwen Goldstein
50 Fuller Brook Rd. • Wellesley, MA 02181 • 617-235-8658

Gwen Goldstein represents professional illustrators catering to the needs of advertising and book publishing. Call today to receive a complete listing of illustrators and the wide variety of styles from cartoon to photo realism offered to handle your special needs. Fax available.

50 Fuller Brook Rd. • Wellesley, MA 02181 • 6 1 7 • 2 3 5 • 8 6 5 8

Jimmy Holder

1507 Columbia Drive
Glendale, California 91205

(818) 244-6707
Fax in studio.

Clients include: Ogilvy & Mather, McCann-Erickson, J. Walter Thompson, Hill, Holliday, Tracy-Locke, IBM, Coca-Cola, Domino's Pizza, Jim Dandy, Dixie Crystals, Alabama Power, Citizen's & Southern National Bank, Atlanta Journal & Constitution, Turner Broadcasting System, Atlanta Braves.

Member Graphic Artists Guild

V. I. B. S

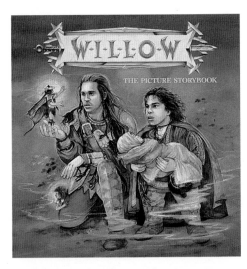

Diane deGroat

BRISTOL PLACE

CHAPPAQUA, NEW YORK 10514

(914) 238-4115

Clients include: American Book, Atheneum, Bradbury, *Chemical Week,* Children's Book Council, Clarion, Clarus Music, *Contemporary Pediatrics,* Crown, Dell, Dial, Dutton, Farrar Straus, Franklin Watts, Ginn, *Good Housekeeping,* Harcourt Brace Jovanovich, Harper & Row, *Highlights,* Holt, *Home,* Houghton Mifflin, Knopf, *Ladybug,* Lothrop, Lucasfilm, McGraw-Hill, Macmillan, Medical Economics, Morrow, North American Bear, Orchard, Putnam, Random House, Reader's Digest, *RN,* Robert Wood Johnson Foundation, Scholastic, Scribners, Seabury, Simon & Schuster, South Street Seaport, Sudler & Hennessy, Troll, Viking, Warne.

Dave Joly

15 KING STREET
PUTNAM, CT 06260

(203) 928-1042
FAX (203) 928-1238

Gary Hovland

3408 Crest Drive

Manhattan Beach, CA 90266

(310) 545-6808

Clients include: the New York Times, Conde Nast Traveler, Sierra, Newsweek, Time, Business Week, the Washington Post, the Los Angeles Times, the Chicago Tribune, Scholastic Inc., Alfred A. Knopf, Simon & Schuster, Ogilvy & Mather Advertising, and Grey Advertising.

Darren Ching
312 East 6th Street, Apt. C-3
New York, NY 10003

(212) 254-0963

Clients include: Contraband Dance
Theater, Elbows Akimbo Theater
Group, IBM, NC Press, New York
Times, San Francisco Bay Guardian,
The Julian Theater, Viz Comics, Watch
Magazine.

Norman RAINOCK
804·264·8123

Patrick Kelley

1127 California
Grand Rapids, MI 49504
(616) 459-7540

Specializing in: Editorial,
Humorous Editorial,
and Portraiture.

Member of the
Graphic Artists Guild

Also Featured in
*American Artists:
an Illustrated Survey
of Leading Contemporaries*

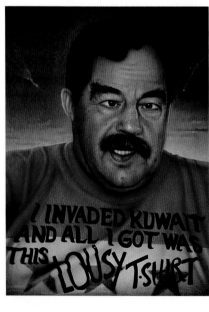

Janet Pietrobono   Member Graphic Artists Guild

SIDE DOOR STUDIO
342 LEXINGTON AVENUE
MOUNT KISCO, NEW YORK 10549

(914) 666-3001

Tom Durfee

66 Broadway
San Francisco, CA 94111

(415) 781-0527

Animation reel available.

Thomas Amorosi
Teresa Amorosi

INTAGLIO DIMENSION
6 COMPTON STREET
EAST ROCKAWAY, NEW YORK 11518
STUDIO (516) 596-0160
MESSAGES (516) 593-3845

Color and Black & White conceptual, editorial, product, medical and scientific illustration. Work appears in American Showcase 14 & 15, Illustrators 33 and 1991 Medical Illustration Source Book.

Clients: Insurance Review; Cosmopolitan; Magic Moments, Inc.; Sunshine Studios; Annual Review Inc. (Anthropology); Hunter College, CUNY; New York University; Bryn Mawr College.

Awards: Society of Illustrators 33rd Annual National Exhibition. Affiliations: Graphic Artists Guild Association of Medical Illustrators Guild of Natural Science Illustrators

Glenn Harrington

Represented by

Barbara Gordon Associates

165 East 32nd Street

New York, New York 10016

(212) 686-3514

Studio (215) 294-8104

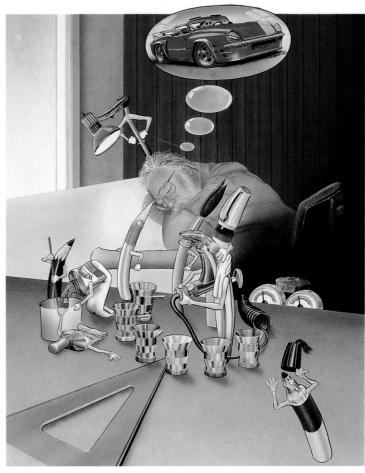

Lou Byer
Kennie Hill

MERIDIAN DESIGN STUDIO, INC.
3590 NORTH MERIDIAN
INDIANAPOLIS, IN 46208

(317) 925-8333

Meridian Design Studio principals, Lou Byer and Keni Hill, are the creative energies behind these examples of quality illustration. We believe our work speaks for itself and our client list will attest to that. Clients include: Detroit Diesel Allison, Elanco, RCA, EMS Laboratories, Indiana Pacers, Delco, Cadillac/Olds Div. of G.M., Eli Lilly, White Arts, Sander Communications, Transglow Systems of Ontario, King Sports, Engine Essentials, Steak N' Shake, Young & Rubicam, General Tire, Farm Bureau Co-Op, P&C Media, Spitzer Race Cars, Groff Motor Sports, Takenaka Int'l. U.S.A., Howard Sams, IVY Tech, P.R. Duke, Saturday Evening Post, Herff Jones, Master Software, Xerox Corp.

Does this remind you of what it's like building an application to manage complex data?

More than fare.

Special Offer For People Who Commute To Work in Downtown Ann Arbor

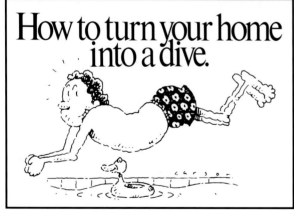

How to turn your home into a dive.

Jim Carson

11 Foch Street

Cambridge, MA 02140

(617) 661-3321

Lots of clients.

Lots of awards.

Lots of experience.

Fax in studio. FedEx at the door.

My portfolio loves to travel. It can be on your desk tomorrow morning.

Bob Crōmb

Bringing the fun back to illustration

45 Lorraine Road, Island Park, NY 11558   (516) 432 - 4463

Bill Russell
949 Filbert Street #5
San Francisco, California 94133

(415) 474-4159

Scratchboard illustration for all applications.

Partial list of clients includes: Archeology Magazine, Book-of-the-Month Club; Boston Globe; Canadian Airlines; Condé-Nast Publications; Case for Advertising; Esquire; FYI; General Motors; Harrowsmith; Husk, Jennings, Advertising; Inx; The Kelly Group; Lotus Magazine; Modern Maturity; New York Life Insurance Co.; Outside; Penguin, U.S.A.; Prentice-Hall Press; Premiere; Saatchi & Saatchi Advertising; Time-Life Promotion; Walking Magazine; The Wall Street Journal; The Washington Post Magazine; Whittle Communications; Wig Wag.

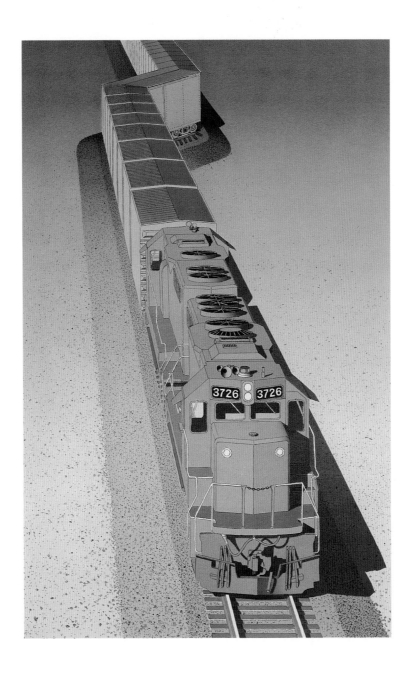

Guy Billout

A THOUSAND WORDS, INC.
225 LAFAYETTE STREET, SUITE 1008
NEW YORK, NY 10012-4015

(212) 431-6350

Clients:

Magazines: Fortune, Glamour, Life, New York, The Atlantic Monthly, The New York Times, Playboy, Vogue.

Annual Reports: Comcast, Gard, GATX Capital Corporation, Hammermill, Met-ropolitan Life, Micom, San Francisco International Airport, Schlumberberger, People's Bank.

Advertising Campaigns: Baxter Travenol, Burlington Northern, First Boston, Logicon, Mutual of Omaha, Nielsen, Northern Telecom, Reemtsma (Germany), Westminster Bank (U.K.).

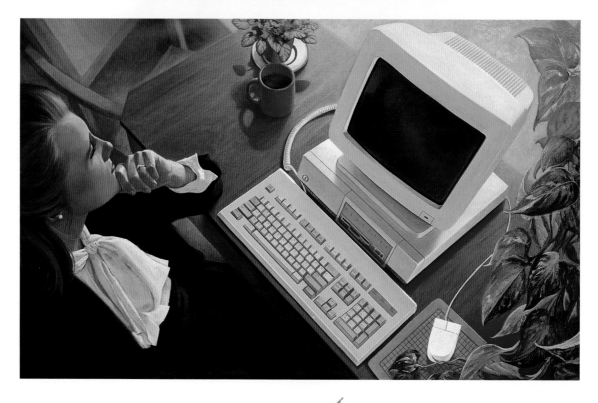

bruce bowles

Studio   415   731 - 4084   2140   Nineteenth   Avenue   San Francisco   California   94116   Fax   415   566 - 8928

The Moon Is Following Me
by Philip Heckman
illustrated by Mary O'Keefe Young

Something Magic
by Maggie S. Davis
illustrated by Mary O'Keefe Young

Mary O'Keefe Young

62 MIDCHESTER AVENUE
WHITE PLAINS, NY 10606

(914) 949-0147
FAX AVAILABLE.

Additional work may be seen in
American Showcase 12, 13, 14.

Member Graphic Artists Guild

Watercolor and Pastel Illustrations

Commissioned Portraits also available.

Clients include: Abbott Labs, Allison
Greetings, Atheneum, Bozell Inc.,
Caswell Massey, C.R. Gibson, Country
Journal, Crown, Dodd Mead, Dye-
ables, Easter Seals, Harcourt Brace

Jovanovich, Macmillan, Scholastic,
Simon and Schuster.

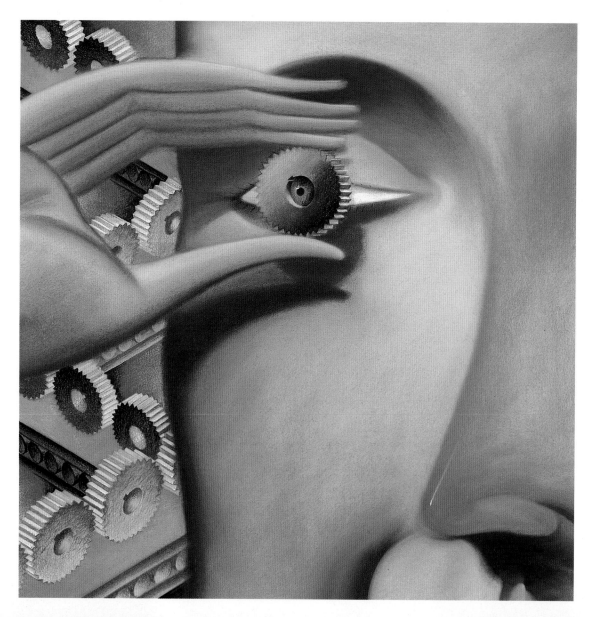

Keith D. Skeen

KEITH D. SKEEN ILLUSTRATION
3228 PRAIRIE DRIVE
DEERFIELD, WI 53531

(608) 423-3020

Client list: Anaquest, Dynatech/Color-graphics, G.E. Corporate, Kohler Co., Pleasant Co., Promega Biotech, Prime Times Magazine, Runner's World Magazine, Snap-On Tools Inc., The United Way, The Washington Post, The Wisconsin Department of Tourism.

Awards: Flash Creative Print and Advertising, 1990/Gold; Children's Reading Round Table of Chicago, 1987, 1988, Honor.

© NSI VIDEO 1990

© OCEAN PACIFIC 1990

SCOTT Angle

21051 BARBADOS CIRCLE
HUNTINGTON BEACH
CALIFORNIA 92646

PHONE

7 1 4

9 6 0

8 4 8 5

POLLY M. LAW
305-A PRESIDENT
BROOKLYN, NY 11231
TEL: 718·875·4425
FAX: 718·858·4617

COMPS

& STORYBOARDS

POLLY M. LAW
305-A PRESIDENT
BROOKLYN, NY 11231
TEL: 718·875·4425
FAX: 718·858·4617

ANIMATICS

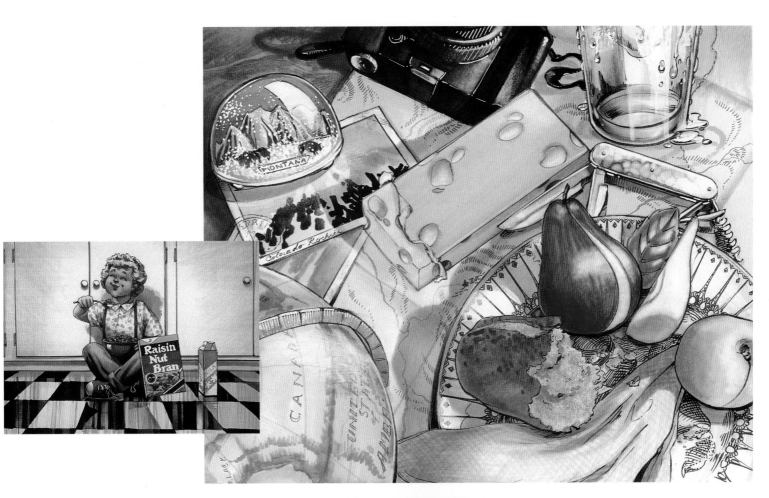

& STORYBOARDS

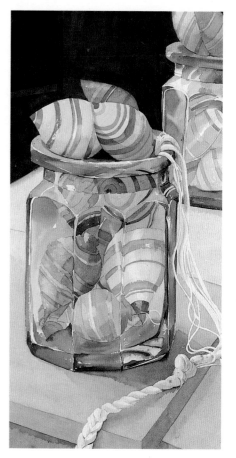

Leyla Torres

718.389.6101 • 14 North Henry Street, Brooklyn NY 11222

Mary Ross

MARY ROSS ILLUSTRATION
508 CLAYTON STREET
SAN FRANCISCO, CA 94117

(415) 431-2109

Mary Ross has been drawing whimsical, wiggley characters for over a decade. Clients include: Chevron Corporation, Pacific Bell, Hewlett-Packard, Levi-Strauss as well as many smaller companies.

The dog and pony show, above, was created for Edwin Schwartz, Public Relations, San Francisco.

A STAR
IS BORN

Marc Rosenthal

#8 ROUTE 66
MALDEN BRIDGE, NY 12115

PHONE/FAX (518) 766-4191

Clients include: Altman & Manley/
Eagle Advertising, Fortune, Time,
Newsweek, U.S. News & World Report,
Playboy, New York Magazine, Vanity
Fair, AT&T, Whittle Communications,
The Boston Globe, The Washington
Post, The New York Times, The Phila-
delphia Inquirer.

Rosemary Salvatore
232 NORTH AVENUE, SUITE 111
NEW ROCHELLE, NY 10801

(914) 636-6269

I work primarily in cut-paper.

Member of the Graphic Artists Guild.

Clients include: Recycled Paper Products, Vermont T's, and The Mary Imogene Bassett Hospital.

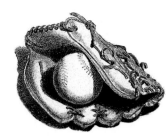

**Karen Meyer
Swearingen**

36-B MARRINER AVE.
ALBANY, NY 12205

(518) 482-3207

Finely rendered, light filled pencil
drawings for editorial, advertising and
children's books.

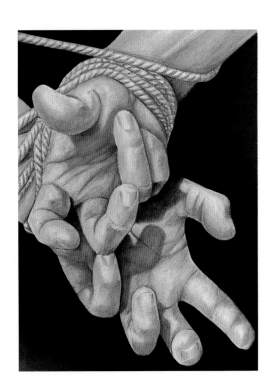

Paul Hamill

PAUL HAMILL ILLUSTRATION
1009 EMPEY WAY
SAN JOSE, CALIFORNIA 95128

(408) 280-0879

Specializing in graphite pencil drawings with watercolor washes.

Clients include: Atari Corporation, G.T.E. Government Systems, Kaiser Permanente, Ibis Software, Acer Computers, Symantec, Asian American Manufacturing Association, Samco, Deals on Wheels, Starburst Construction, Sources 1990, Devasoft.

John A. Lytle

LYTLE STUDIO
17130 YOSEMITE ROAD
P.O. BOX 5155
SONORA, CA 95370

(209) 928-4849

Additional illustrations may be seen in American Showcase 5–7, 10–15; Art Directors Index 10, 11; Adweek Portfolio 1986; GAG Directory of Illustration 5, 7.

Clients include: ABC Sports, American Express, AT&T, Bank of America, CBS Sports, Edelbrock, Eli Lilly, Goodyear, Hewlett Packard, Jaguar, Levi-Strauss, Nike, New York Telephone, NFL Films, PG&E, Reebok, R.J. Reynolds, Ryder Trucks, Seagrams, Sheraton, Sperry, Squirt, Visa, Yamaha Motorcycles.

Member Society of Illustrators.

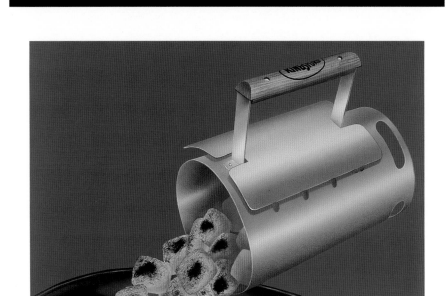

Mark Schroeder

66 Broadway
San Francisco, CA 94111

(415) 421-3691

Member Society of Illustrators,
San Francisco.

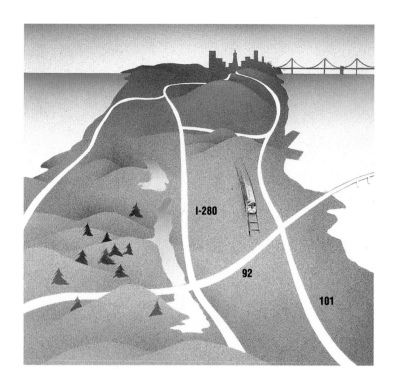

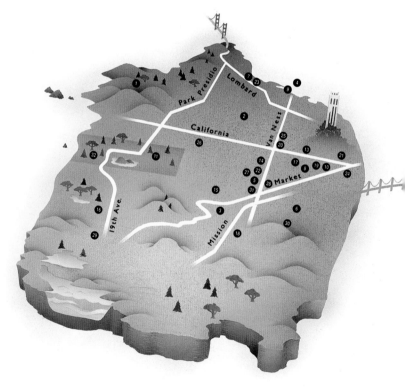

Karen Minot

KAREN MINOT ILLUSTRATION
26 DEUCE COURT
FAIRFAX, CALIFORNIA 94930

(415) 457-7559

With my unique approach to maps, my clients have enjoyed the new opportunities they have to make a traditionally dry item come to life. My maps have been used as insets to more technical and directional maps as well as just by themselves. They have wonderful applications on printed pieces for universities, cities, travel, special events, transportation, recreation. Please call for additional samples or to discuss your particular needs.

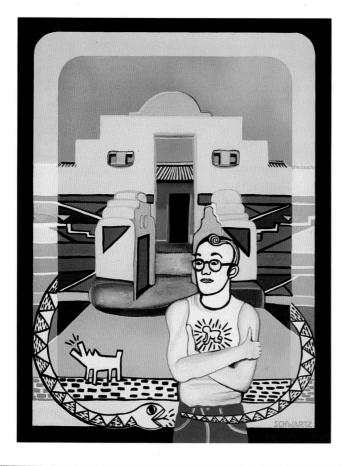

Judith Schwartz

231 East 5th Street, No. 6
New York, NY 10003

(212) 777-7533
Fax in studio

Clients include: *Travel Holiday, Business Week, Cosmopolitan Magazine, PC Magazine,* C.M.P. Publications, Inc., W.H. Freeman, D.M.S. Systems Inc., National Investor Data Services, Flying Point Software, Long Island University, South Street Seaport Museum, Staten Island Children's Museum, The Working Women's Institute, Federal Bar Council, East Shore Broadcasting.

Work can also be seen in: Graphic Artists Guild Directory 6, RSVP 17 (1992 edition).

• Member Graphic Artists Guild
• Graduate of Cooper Union
• Adjunct Professor, Long Island University/Southampton Campus

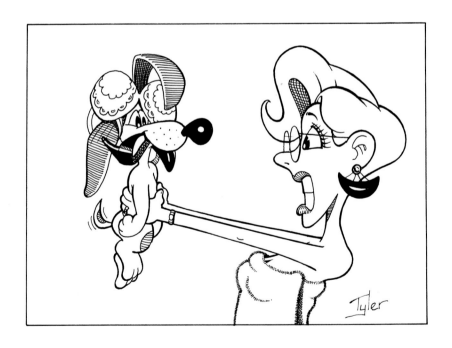

Craig Tyler
2691 Hurricane Cove
Port Hueneme, CA 93041

(805) 984-3485

Lynne Prentice
2691 Hurricane Cove
Port Hueneme, CA 93041

(805) 984-0013

Rod Thomas

157 LANGLEY ROAD
NEWTON CENTRE, MA 02159

PHONE & FAX (617) 244-2393

Lower Left: Golf Shop Operations
Magazine
Lower Right: Digital Review

Clients include: Boston Magazine; Inc.
Magazine; Data General; CVS; New Age
Journal; PC Week; Cosmopolitan; DC
Heath; Houghton Mifflin; Cahners
Publishing; Yankee Publishing; Silver
Burdett & Ginn; CMP Publications.

Sue Ellen Brown

(214) 823-9545

REPRESENTED BY NANCY LEWIS
(214) 520-2185
FAX AVAILABLE.

- Exciting illustrations that meet client demand.
- Unlimited subjects: people, animals, products, and packaging.
- Full range of styles: airbrush, realistic, humorous, animated, and

- Twelve years experience.
- Numerous awards.

Current clients: Sears; Dr. Pepper; Frito-Lay; Atheneum Publishers; Jack Tar Village; Baylor University Medical

MD&A; Claypoole, Burk & Hummel; Brandywine Art.

Laura Freeman
208 East 34th Street, #4A
New York, NY 10016

(212) 679-0812

Joe Jusko
15 Mobile Avenue
Staten Island, NY 10306

(718) 979-3064

List of clients includes: LMR/RCA
Records; Marvel Comics; Island
Records, London; Titansports, Inc./
World Wrestling Federation; Remco
Toys; Allegiance Records; Topps Trad-
ing Cards; NFL; Heavy Metal Magazine.

TIM LUNDGREN
ILLUSTRATION

Timothy A. Lundgren

TIM LUNDGREN • ILLUSTRATION
4200 TORRINGFORD STREET
TORRINGTON, CONNECTICUT 06790

(203) 496-7439

1980 graduate of the Rhode Island School of Design with a B.F.A. in Illustration. From 1981–82 lived and worked in New York City doing children's textbook illustrations. From 1982–90 lived and worked in Providence, Rhode Island doing illustrations, primarily in pen & ink, for advertising agencies in the Providence-Boston area. Returned to hometown of Torrington, Connecticut in March of 1991 and am working with clients from a much wider region of the country. Specialize in traditional pen & ink illustration. Subject matter: people, situations, landscapes, seascapes, animals, etc.

Dave Clegg
3571 Aaron Sosebee Road
Cumming, Georgia 30130

(404) 887-6306
Fax (404) 781-5780

Represented by Susan Wells
(404) 255-1430
Fax (404) 255-3449
5134 Timber Trail, N.E.
Atlanta, Georgia 30342

Abramowitz

401 East 80th Street, Suite 23K
New York, New York 10021

(212) 570-6629

Individual and Corporate Fine Art,
Textile and Graphic Illustration

Partial list of clients:
Philadelphia Zoo
Jersey Wildlife Preservation Trust,
 Channel Islands, British Isles
Getex, Inc.
Zambia Airways
S.O.S. Animals

Trans World Airlines
Jolie Gabor—designs for Diamond
 Perfume Scarf
New Northern Brokerage, Fine Art
 Insurers

Abramowitz

401 EAST 80TH STREET, SUITE 23K
NEW YORK, NEW YORK 10021

(212) 570-6629

WATERHOLE

The most recent release created by wildlife specialist Abramowitz reinforces the artist's tribute to the animal kingdom, representing all that is beautiful in nature . . . filled with love and warmth . . . to be protected and cherished.

"NEVER TO BECOME SIMPLY A VALUABLE MEMORY, BUT TO BE PRESERVED FOR ALWAYS . . . FOR EVERYONE."

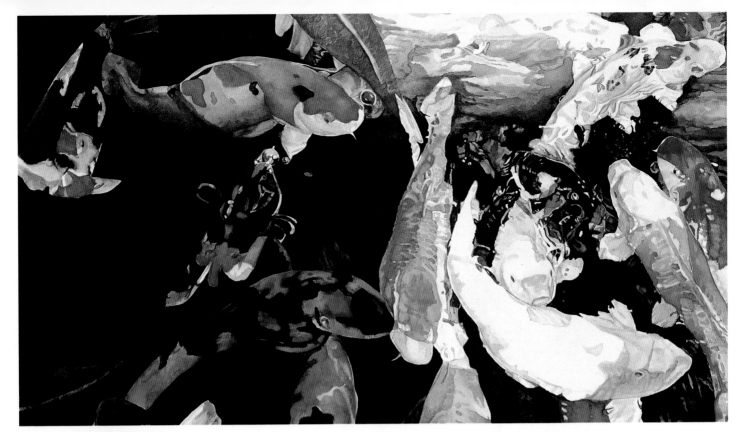

Patti Gay

1243 TERRA NOVA BLVD.
PACIFICA, CALIFORNIA 94044

(415) 359-5608

Client List:
Group W Cable
Marcel Schurman Co. Inc.
Potpourri Press
Sunrise Publications
Peninsula Humane Society
Western Visions Gallery

Gibson Greeting Cards
Bentley House Limited
Red Farm Studio

Mary K. Thelen
5907 LLANO
DALLAS, TEXAS 75206

(214) 827-8073
FAX SERVICE AVAILABLE.

Clients include: DLM Publishing; Hall-mark Cards, Inc.; Holt, Rinehart and Winston; Gibson Greetings, Inc.; Macmillan/McGraw-Hill Publishing, Ogilvy & Mather Advertising; Sangamon, Inc., Scott-Foresman, Inc.; Southwestern

Bell; Susan Crane, Inc.; Weekly Reader Corp.; Albert Whitman and Co.

Represented by
Jerry Leff Associates, Inc.
Tel: 212-697-8525
Fax: 212-949-1843

Member:
Graphic Artists Guild
Dallas Society of Illustrators
Society of Children's Book Writers

Tony De Luz

TONY DE LUZ STUDIO
49 MELCHER STREET
BOSTON, MA 02210

(617) 695-0006
FAX IN STUDIO

Realistic illustration in watercolor and
pencil on a variety of subjects.

Member Graphic Artists Guild.

Stephen Silvestri

STEPHEN SILVESTRI DESIGN
79-43 69TH AVENUE
MIDDLE VILLAGE, NY 11379

(718) 326-0193

Type illustration, design and all forms
of lettering.

Member, Graphic Artists Guild.

award winning Illustrations for Advertising & Design?

1905 WEST FOSTER
CHICAGO,
ILLINOIS 60640
312 • 728 • 2738

RICHARD SYSKA ILLUSTRATION DESIGN

Fax Available

Matt Baier

214/216 Avenue A, #2D
New York, NY 10009

(212) 228-1143

Clients include:
Performance
High Times
Kick

THE HEREAFTER GANG

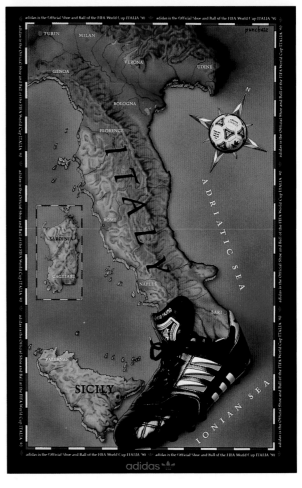

Don Ivan Punchatz

2605 WESTGATE DRIVE
ARLINGTON, TX 76015

(817) 469-8151 METRO
(817) 468-9377 FAX

Represented by:
Darwin Bahm
(212) 989-7074
(212) 627-0863 FAX

Bob Bahm
(216) 398-1338

"For more than 25 years, I've completed assignments for practically *every* major national ad agency, magazine, publishing house and record company. Many of these illustrations have also won top awards in major professional shows.

I enjoy the challenge of developing concepts for my clients or taking their ideas to completion under tight deadline schedules if necessary . . . and my prices are competitive. Please call my agents for specific samples or bids. Thanks!"

SPIECE GRAPHICS

219 - 747 - 3916

1811 WOODHAVEN #7

P.O. BOX 9115

FT. WAYNE, IN 46899

HAND LETTERING

TITLES

PACKAGE GRAPHICS

LOGOS

LETTER DESIGN

APPLE MACINTOSH®

COMPUTER, FAX

AND MODEM IN

STUDIO

MEMBER GRAPHIC

ARTISTS GUILD

ABCDEF

100% Colombian Coffee

PARK 13 NORTH

CHIPPERS

COLONIAL

OK

WILL BUSH RAISE YOUR TAXES?

U.S.News & WORLD REPORT

MAY 21, 1990 $1.95

THE OLD WEST

THE NEW VIEW OF FRONTIER LIFE

Fading legends: Buffalo Bill, Pawnee Bill, Buffalo Jones

World Cruise

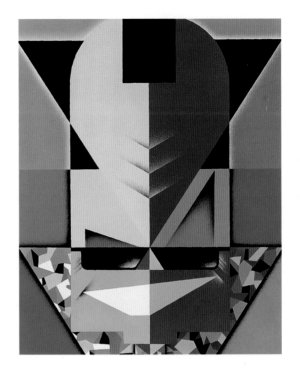

frequent flyer

esquire

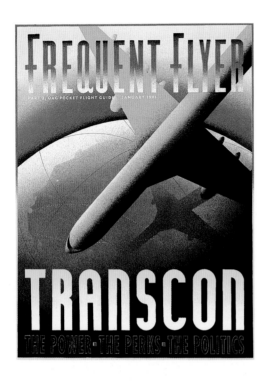

american health

the society of publication designers

164 daniel low terrace si ny 10301

(718) 727 0723   fax (718) 727 0927

the boston globe magazine

the daily news magazine

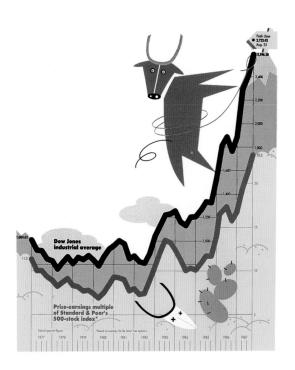

fortune

rolling stone

Renee

Klein

164 daniel low terrace si ny 10301   *(212) 522 4464   or   (718) 727 0723*

STAR-KIST PET FOODS

AT&T

MILTON BRADLEY CO.

DANIELLE
JONES
416·968·6277

Illustration of a Humorous Nature

DANIELLE
JONES
416 · 968 · 6277

Illustration of a Humorous Nature

Bryna Waldman

REPRESENTED BY LEE FISHBACK
350 WEST 21ST STREET #5
NEW YORK, NY 10011

(212) 929-2951

NICK GAETANO

HARVEY KAHN   212 752 8490

FAX 212 753 1721
14 EAST 52 STREET NEW YORK NY 10022

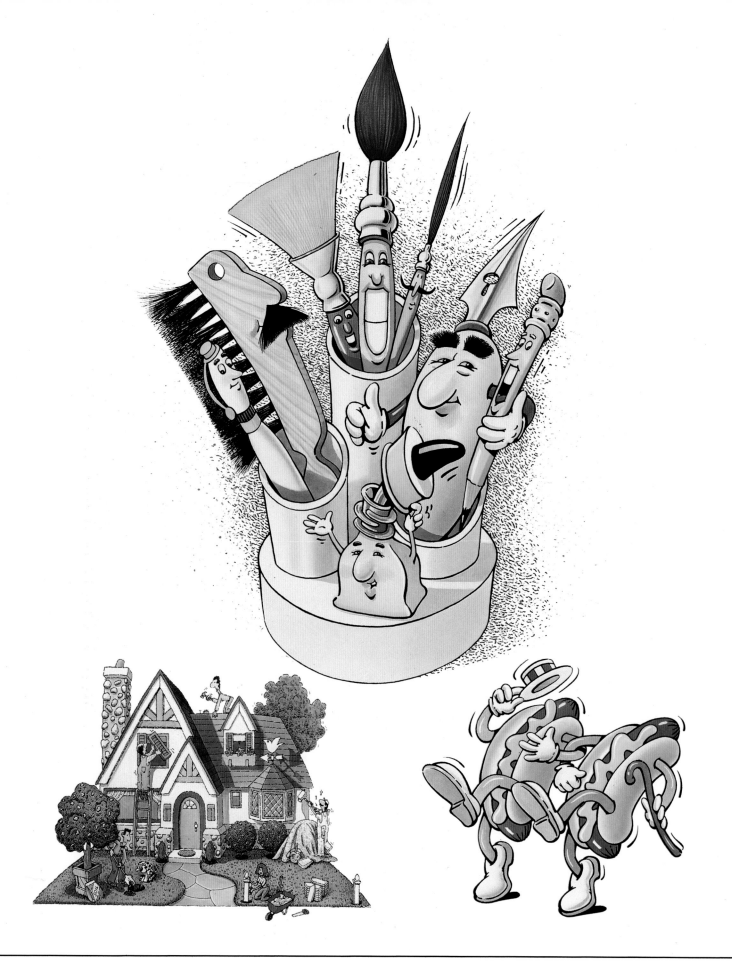

Bob Brugger
1930 ROBINSON STREET
REDONDO BEACH, CA 90278

(213) 372-0135
(STARTING JUNE 1992,
USE AREA CODE 310)

Represented by:
Martha Productions, Inc.
(213) 204-1771

Clients include: am/pm, Arco, Caesar's
Tahoe, CBS, Honda, Knott's Berry
Farm, Mattel, McDonald's, NBC, Price
Stern Sloan, Sheraton Hotels, South-
land Corporation, Tomy Toys, TRW,
Vestron Video, Warner Bros.

MARK RIEDY

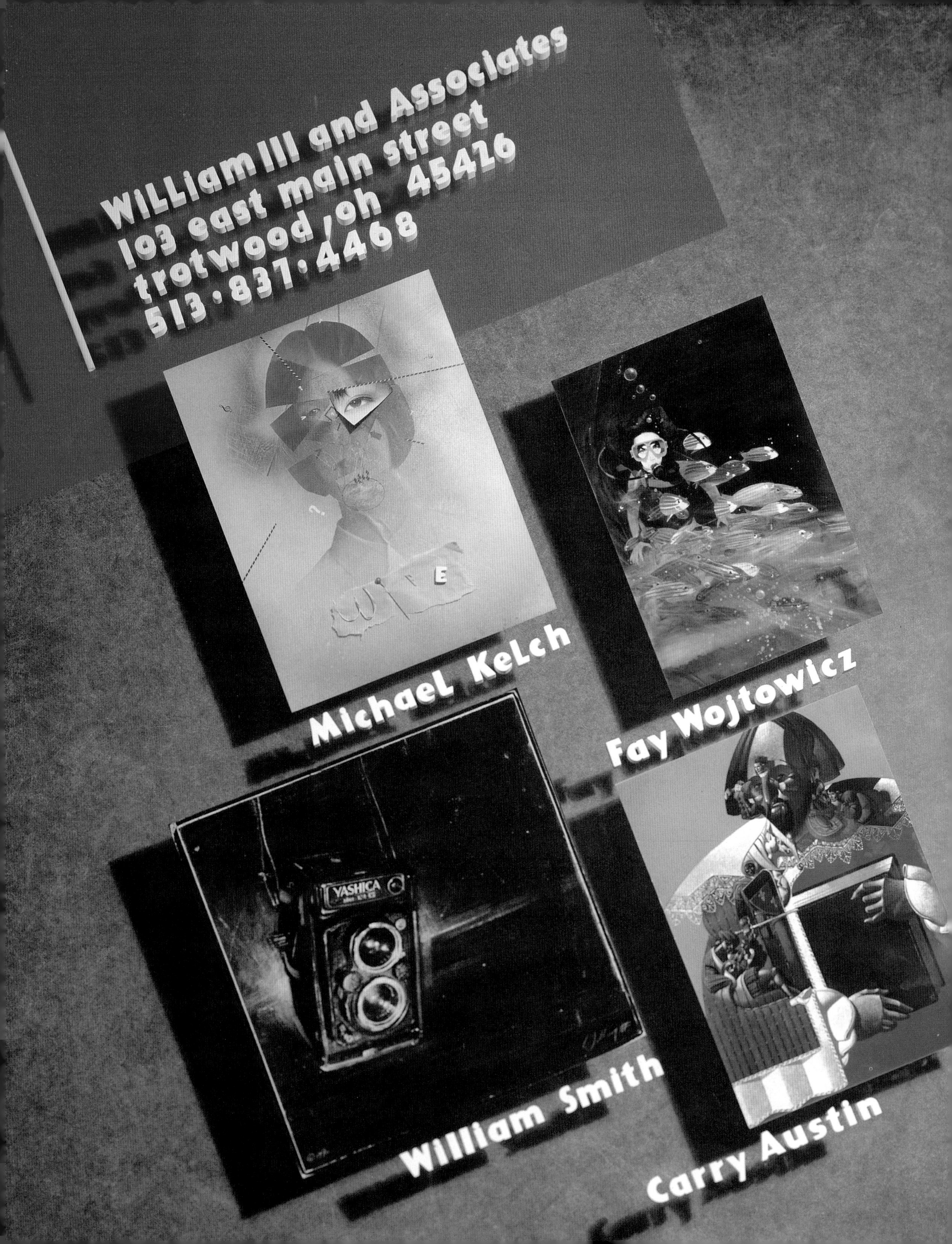
WiLLiam III and Associates
103 east main street
trotwood,oh 45426
513·837·4468
MichaeL KeLch
Fay Wojtowicz
William Smith
Carry Austin
YASHICA

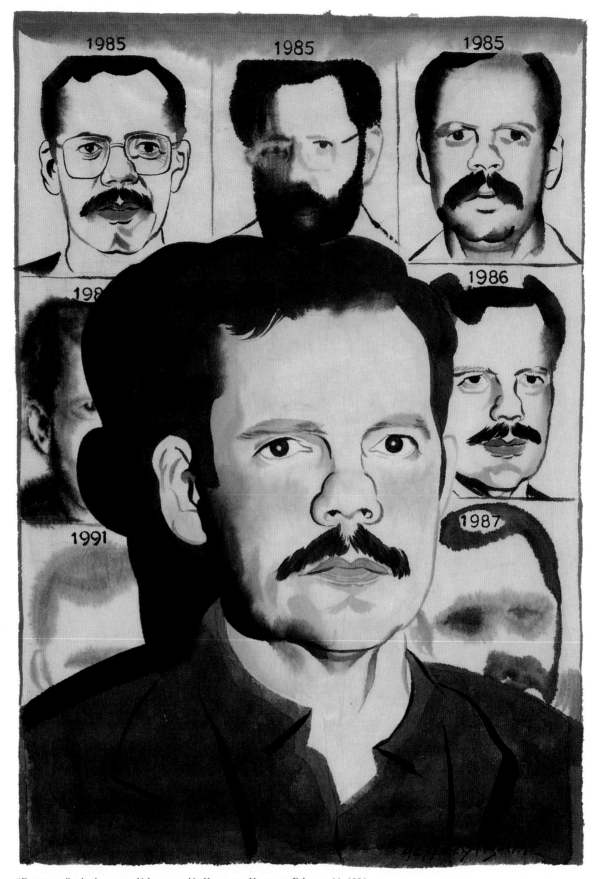

"FORGOTTEN" a book excerpt which appeared in NEWSWEEK MAGAZINE, February 11, 1991

JEFFREY SMITH

7 West Street, Warwick, New York 10990 Tel 914 986 1020 Fax 914 986 1033

*One of one hundred and fifty illustrations produced for "P*EACHBOY*", A childrens video produced by R*ABBIT *E*ARS *I*NC.

*"F*ORGOTTEN*" a book excerpt which appeared in N*EWSWEEK *M*AGAZINE*, February 11, 1991*

JEFFREY SMITH

7 West Street, Warwick, New York 10990 Tel 914 986 1020 Fax 914 986 1033

Big Entertainment, Little Dish.
$1.00 A Day.

PRIMESTAR℠
Distributed by
TCI of Arkansas, Inc.
1-800-932-2007

Cathy Morrison

BIG CHIEF GRAPHICS
775 E. PANAMA DRIVE
LITTLETON, CO 80121

(303) 798-0424
FAX (303) 797-1403

Clients include:

American Cancer Society
American Express
American Television
  & Communications
Children's Hospital
Gerry Baby Products

HBO
Mountain Bell
Tele-Communications, Inc.

JOHN KANE

215·862·0392

9 West Bridge St, New Hope, PA 18938

Van Howell

P.O. Box 812
Huntington, New York 11743

Studio phone & Fax: (516) 424-6499

246

Partial client list: Random House, Doubleday, Morrow, Macmillan, Schocken, Newsday, Wall Street Journal, American Banker, DLJ, AdWeek, WQXR, Medical Economics, Eyetooth Design, Marvel, DDB Needham, AC&R, DMB&B, Y&R, Grey Advertising.

Silver Award from Society of Newspaper Design, merit awards from Society of Illustrators.

Portraits & caricatures of figures in politics, sports and high & low culture, in a broad range of moods and styles.

Ted Sokolowski

TED SOKOLOWSKI ILLUSTRATIONS
R.D. #2 Box 408
LAKE ARIEL, PA 18436

(717) 937-4527
FAX IN STUDIO.

Upper left: Practical Homeowner
Magazine.

Lower Center: Foote, Cone & Belding/
Zenith

©Ted Sokolowski 1991

Call for additional samples in B&W
and color, or client list.

Member Graphic Artists Guild.

MATT FOSTER

6766 SNOWDON AVENUE
EL CERRITO, CA 94530
510.215.1251 / CALL FOR FAX

MATT FOSTER

6766 SNOWDON AVENUE
EL CERRITO, CA 94530
510.215.1251 / CALL FOR FAX

Peter Bono
114 EAST SEVENTH STREET
CLIFTON, NJ 07011-1134

(201) 340-1169
FAX (201) 772-5178

I'll originate concepts
or work with your design.
TOP LEFT: FORBES, article about the
perils of partnerships.
TOP RIGHT: JVB ADVERTISING, D.M.
piece about cereal packaging.

MIDDLE LEFT: Caricature of Ted
Kennedy
MIDDLE: KOUGH ASSOCIATES
MIDDLE RIGHT: US MAGAZINE, article
on Republican politics.
BOTTOM: MADISON AVENUE, article
about bank deregulation.

CLIENTS: AT&T, Dow Jones, J. Walter
Thompson, McCann Direct, NBC,
Ogilvy & Mather, Saatchi & Saatchi,
Steve Phillips.
Barron's, Business Week, Discover,
Family Circle, Field & Stream, Inside

Sports, Newsweek, People, Playboy,
Reader's Digest.
EXHIBITED: Society of Illustrators

SHAY COHEN

ILLUSTRATION
011 • 972 • 52 • 574 090
4 1 5 • 8 9 3 7 3 5 5

Nestle Food, Hills Bros., Kraft General Foods, Knudsen,
Beatrice/ Hunt- Wesson, Orville Redenbacher, Quaker Oats,
Ocean Spray, Sunshine Cookies, Calavo Growers, Sunsweet Growers
Heublein, Capri Sun, Mothers Cookies, Gallo Vineyards, The Wine Group,
Shaklee, Carnation, Goelitz, Primo Angeli, Etc.

Tony Capparelli

TONY CAPPARELLI ILLUSTRATIONS
110 CLAIRMONT AVENUE
WESTWOOD, NJ 07675

(201) 358-1536
(914) 352-4354

Client list: L&F Products, Medical Economics, N.J. Devils Hockey Team, Beecham Products, American Automobile Association, Field & Stream, Becton Dickinson, National Review, Proctor & Gamble, Scholastic, Ski Magazine, Performance Marketing Group, Multimedia-Sports Media, Nabisco, U.S. Postal Service, Wunderman Worldwide.

Magazine Covers: National Review, Financial World, Drug Topics, N.J. Devils Yearbook, Contemporary Pediatrics, Contemporary OBGYN.

Package Illustration: Lysol, Love My Carpet, Direct, Bauer & Black, Ace, Aqua Fresh For Kids, Diaparene, Sine-Aid.
Awards: Professional Hockey Writers Award for Yearbooks; Art Direction Magazine Certificate of Distinction.

Clients include:
Washington Post
Boston Globe
New York Times
Entertainment Weekly
MS.
Stuff Magazine
Esprit
Apple Computer
Lotus
Digital
AT&T
MTV
Polaroid
Harvard University
etc.

POLO BARRERA is the answer for your Advertising, Editorial, Publishing and Corporate Identity illustration needs.

617 963•3921 7 Kennedy Dr., Randolph, MA 02368

Marie Masciovecchio

90 GOLD STREET #3J
NEW YORK, NY 10038

(212) 233-3672

Member of Graphic Artists Guild.

Fine art for individual and corporate
clients. Advertising and all medias.
Fax available.

Fall in love again.

With your career, of course. Come to the Graphic Artists
Guild's National Conference, and remember why you got in
the business in the first place. June 11, 12, 13, and 14, 1992, in
Washington, D.C. Call 212.463.7730 for details.

Eye to Eye. Where art gets smart.

EYE♦EYE

GRAPHIC ARTISTS GUILD
NATIONAL CONFERENCE

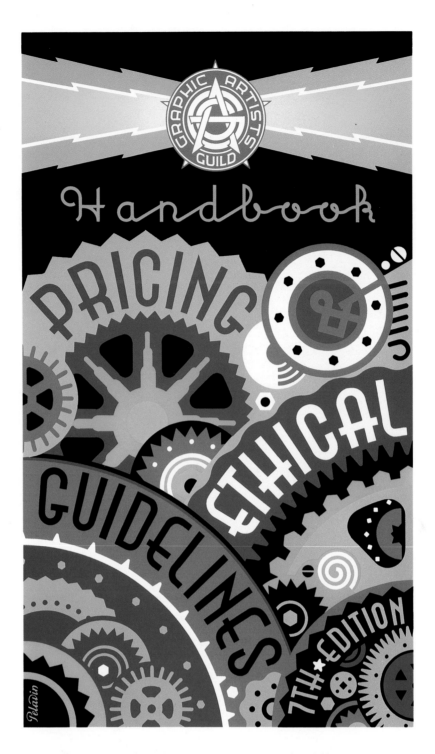

DO IT BY THE BOOK.

HOW DO YOU DECIDE on an appropriate fee for artwork you sell or buy? How do you write a contract that's fair to both artist and buyer? What are the implications of new technologies in the art marketplace? If you're an artist, what business practices should you expect from your clients? And if you're a buyer, what should you expect from a professional artist? ★ ARTISTS AND BUYERS ALIKE will find good answers to questions like these in *Pricing & Ethical Guidelines,* 7th Edition. Published by the Graphic Artists Guild, the *Guidelines* contains the result of the Guild's extensive survey of pricing levels in every branch of the graphic arts, as well as a wealth of information on estimates, proposals, contracts, copyrights, and many other aspects of the business relationship between artist and buyer.

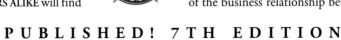

JUST PUBLISHED! 7TH EDITION

TO ORDER YOUR COPY of this indispensable reference, send $22.95 plus 3.50 shipping and handling, along with your name and address, to the **Graphic Artists Guild, 11 West 20th Street, New York, NY 10011-3704.**
New York residents please add 8-1/4% sales tax of $1.89